LONG

English
Works

STUDENTS' BOOK

1

Robert O'Neill

Longman

Longman Group UK Limited,
Longman House, Burnt Mill, Harlow,
Essex CM20 2JE, England
and Associated Companies throughout the world.

First published 1993

Set in 10/11pt ITC Garamond light

Printed in Great Britain
by Cambus Litho

ISBN 0582 08539 X

Designed by Andrew Oliver

Illustrated by: Kathy Baxendale, Ben Campbell,
Sue Faulkes (Eikon Ltd), Robina Green,
Jeremy Oliver, Sam Thompson (Eikon Ltd)
and Gary Wing.

Acknowledgements

We are indebted to IPC Women's Magazines for
permission to reproduce an adapted extract from an
article in *LIVING* Magazine, April 1989, p.63.

The phonetic chart (page 91) and dictionary definitions
throughout are adapted from the *Longman Active Study
Dictionary* and from the *Longman Dictionary of
Contemporary English*.

We are grateful to the following for permission to
reproduce copyright photographs:

Art Directors photo library for page 30 (top left);
Images photo library for page 30 (top right); Network for
page 18 (top left).

All photographs not listed above were taken by
Trevor Clifford/Longman photographer.

Cover photograph by Tony Stone Worldwide.

Special thanks to the following for their help during
location photography:

Barretts, Bishops Stortford; BBC Radio Cambridgeshire;
Duxford Air Museum; Gatwick Airport Ltd; Gatwick
Hilton International; JR's, Bishops Stortford;
Mamma Amalfi, Hatfield; Ristorante Venezia, Bishops
Stortford; Thomas Cook, Bishops Stortford.

All office scene photographs directed by
Sandie Huskinson-Rolfe/Photoseekers.

The author and publishers would like to thank all those
who commented on the manuscript during its
development. In particular, they would like to thank the
following:

Sally Burgess   Patricia Mugglestone
Sally Kennedy   Sue Drake   Guy Heath
Gerry Sweeney   Tessa Blackeby

Contents

Unit number *Themes and functions*	*Grammar*	*Vocabulary and pronunciation*	*Useful phrases and other vocabulary*
5 *(p 30–33)* Describing companies Time Changing arrangements	Past, present and future *was/were*	Time Numbers Present or past	• *The company makes, employs, manufactures, plans to . . .* • *The main office is located in . . .* • *Sales are not very good.* • *I'm afraid . . .* • *I'm terribly sorry.* • *convenient*
6 *(p 34–37)* A day at work Making plans Comparing people and things	Regular and irregular past Comparatives *think so*	*have* 'In between' words Stress	• *She didn't feel very well.* • *have a meeting with . . .* • *What's wrong?* • *I wanted to . . .* • *busy*
7 *(p 38–41)* Telephone calls Asking about flights Dates and numbers Airport announcements Problems and advice	*as/than* *some/any*	Leaving and arriving *see* /h/ **h**ere /æ/ b**a**d or /e/ b**e**d	• *Can you hold?* • *As early as possible.* • *Let's see.* • *have an argument with* • *good friends*
8 *(p 42–45)* Education and previous experience Getting and giving personal information Showing interest	Past Simple Short answers Short questions to show interest	*get* Words with two meanings /g/ **g**et or /dʒ/ **j**et /s/ thi**s** or /z/ i**s**	• *be born in . . .* • *grow up in . . .* • *go to school* • *get a degree* • *leave university* • *get a job* • *specialise in . . .* • *What do you plan to do now?* • *Here's my card.* • *software* • *architect*
9 *(p 46–49)* 'Delicate' questions Asking for and giving advice	*for/ago* *should*	Feelings *say* and *tell* /juː/ **you** odd one out	• *I'm glad we could meet.* • *I hope you understand.* • *It's confidential.* • *polite* • *smile*
10 *(p 50–53)* Giving and taking messages Making requests Talking about the future	*could* *will*	Travel *take* or *go on* *-ing* and *-ed* adjectives /ə/ yest**er**day	• *Would you like to leave a message?* • *as soon as possible* • *away on business* • *urgent*
11 *(p 54–57)* Describing a product Materials	Superlatives Adjectives and adverbs	*lend* or *borrow* Materials *I'll do* or *I do*	• *Just a moment, please.* • *make notes* • *Go on, please.* • *It doesn't work.* • *The quality is unusually high.* • *materials*

Unit number Themes and functions	Grammar	Vocabulary and pronunciation	Useful phrases and other vocabulary
12 (p 58–61) Feelings Talking about ambitions	*have to* *something/anything/nothing*	Feelings Dimensions Stress and weak forms	• *increase sales of . . .* • *It's in my report.* • *His real ambition was to . . .* • *try hard enough*
13 (p 62–65) Money and finance Plans and intentions Describing a company's financial performance	*going to* *that/who/which*	*Money* *make* or *do* *up* or *down* /əʊ/ **mo**ment or /ɒ/ **mo**dern /ʃ/ **sh**e	• *What do you know about their financial situation?* • *They didn't do too well . . .* • *bring out a new product* • *Profits fell/rose.* • *There's nothing to worry about.* • *exact figures*
14 (p 66–69) Talking about a job in detail A letter of application	Present Perfect Progressive *some/any*	Verbs and nouns Words people confuse Verbs and nouns *some*	• *work very closely with . . .* • *I have the impression that . . .* • *I am writing to you on the recommendation of . . .* • *I enclose . . .* • *I look forward to your reply.*
15 (p 70–73) Making a good impression at interviews Things you'd like to do	Present Perfect Simple Three verb forms	*say* or *tell* *make* or *do* Stress Same or different	• *You look worried.* • *All my experience has been in . . .* • *Do you mean I should . . . ?* • *No, of course not.* • *have the wrong effect on . . .* • *make a good impression* • *in case there is a delay*
16 (p 74–77) Making a job offer Asking for opinions Making decisions	Past participles Question tags *seem*	*meet, introduce* and *know* *price, cost* and *value* Weak forms	• *What exactly is all this about?* • *What exactly do you want to . . . ?* • *By the way, . . .* • *I'm not sure.* • *I haven't heard from you for . . .* • *As for myself, . . .* • *offer/ accept a job* • *One of the reasons I am writing now is . . .* • *Let me explain the situation.* • *the financial side* • *advantages*

A Times and places

Review

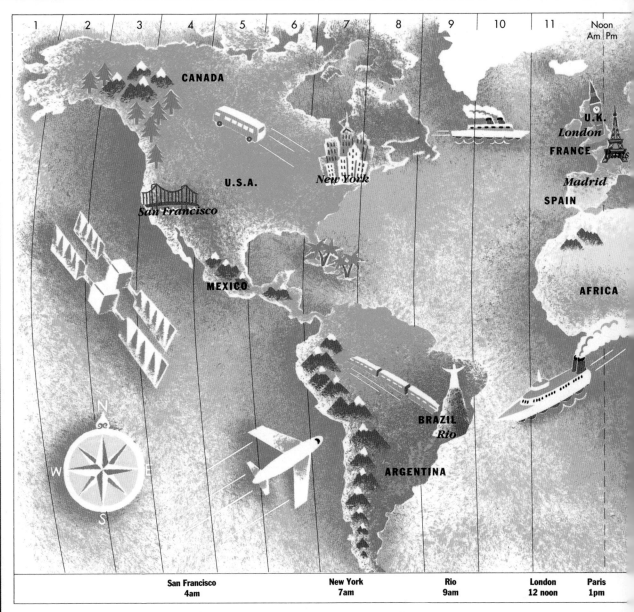

| San Francisco | New York | Rio | London | Paris |
| 4am | 7am | 9am | 12 noon | 1pm |

1

Look at the map. Can you answer these questions?

1 Where is London?
2 Is London a city or a country?
3 What country is Paris in?
4 What time is it in Paris?
5 What time is it in Japan?
6 What is the name of a big city in Japan?
7 What time is it in New York?
8 What time is it in San Francisco?

2 *What about you?*

1 Do you live in San Francisco?
2 What country do you come from?
3 Where do you live now?
4 What time is it now?

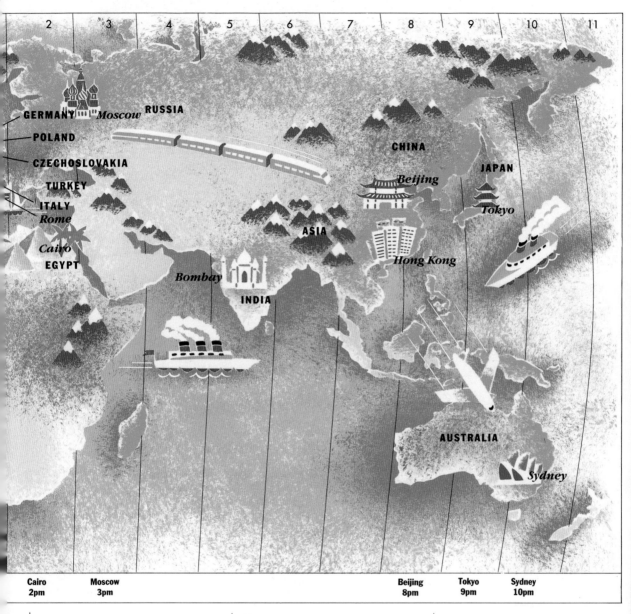

| Cairo | Moscow | | | | | | Beijing | Tokyo | Sydney |
| 2pm | 3pm | | | | | | 8pm | 9pm | 10pm |

3

What is it? A country or a language?

Example: The United States
– a country

1	England	7	English
2	French	8	France
3	Spanish	9	Spain
4	Italy	10	Italian
5	Japan	11	Japanese
6	Greece	12	Greek

4

What language do they speak in these countries?

1 Germany
2 China
3 Russia
4 Turkey
5 Sweden
6 Poland

B Two people

Bay Sports Club

NAME Roger Mitchum

AGE 30

NATIONALITY British

ADDRESS 476 Gonzalez Avenue San Francisco California 94103 U.S.A.

CENTRAL FILM CLUB

Name *Tessa Saunders*

Age *29*

Nationality *British*

Address *12 Greenwood Street Wimbledon London SW19 9DQ England*

1

Look at the information about the characters. Can you answer these questions?

1 What is her name?
2 What is his name?
3 Where does he live?
4 Where does she live?
5 How old is she?
6 How old is he?
7 What is her address?
8 What is his address?
9 What nationality are they?

2 *What about you?*

1 What is your name?
2 What is your address?
3 What nationality are you?

3 *Groupwork*

Ask other people these questions.

What's your name?

Where are you from?

What's your address?

Vocabulary

4

Find the word that doesn't belong.

Example: Spain Rome Brazil Japan
– Rome
1 Russian France German Japanese
2 Monday Wednesday March Friday
3 August Sunday May July
4 month winter spring summer
5 money time dollars yen
6 good fine wonderful bad

Conversation 📼

A man is at a hotel in Tokyo.

A: Good evening, sir. Can I help you?

B: Yes, my name is Mitchum. I have a reservation.

A: Pardon? Can you repeat your name, please?

B: Mitchum.

A: How do you spell that, sir?

B: M...I...T...C...H...U...M.

A: And your first name, please?

B: Roger.

A: Robert? Robert Mitchum?

B: No, Roger. R...O...G...E...R.

A: I'm sorry. Roger. Not Robert. Um... yes, here it is...1st March...Roger Mitchum. A single room with a shower for three nights. Is that right?

B: Yes. From the first to the fourth.

A: Can I see your passport, please?

B: Here you are.

A: Thank you. Your room number is three forty-seven, Mr Mitchum. Here's your key.

B: Thank you.

1 *Writing*

Fill in the form with information about Roger.

SURNAME —————————————

FIRST NAME ————————————

DATE OF ARRIVAL ————————

DATE OF DEPARTURE ——————

ROOM NUMBER —————————

SINGLE ☐ DOUBLE ☐ SHOWER ☐ BATH ☐

2 *What about you?*

1 What is your first name?

2 How do you spell that?

3 What is your surname?

4 How do you spell that?

3

How do you spell these names?

- Rogers • Ríos • Richter • Pirelli • Artaud
- Constantinides • Yamada • Stavitska

4

Say the room numbers.

Three forty-seven

 347

Twelve nineteen

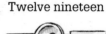 1219

Two fourteen

214

One oh six

106

5

Can you say these room numbers, too?

1 734 2 1921 3 561 4 609 5 906 6 1405

1

Look at the picture and answer these questions.

1 How many people can you see here?
2 Where are two of the people sitting?
3 What are they doing?
4 Find these things in the picture. Give a number.

Example: a poster
– three

- a clock
- a table
- some pencils
- a box with some brochures in it

5 What are the other things you can see
a) on the table?
b) on the wall?
c) on the floor?

6 What is the other man (11) wearing?

2

Look at the pictures below. Which one do you think is a symbol for *in*? Which one is a symbol for *on*? What about *behind*, *in front of*, *near* and *between*?

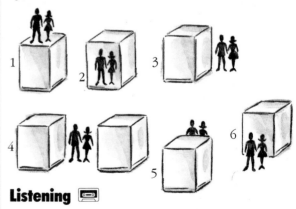

Listening

3

Look at the picture. Listen to the sentences. Which ones are true? Which are false?

Example: The pencils are on the table.
– True.

E Jobs

1

Look at the pictures. Then answer these questions.

Picture one
1 Where are the people in the picture?
2 What are they doing?
3 Do you work in a factory?

Picture two
1 Is that a factory?
2 What is it?
3 What are the people doing?
4 Do you work in an office?

• Now ask questions about pictures three and four.

2

Find the word that doesn't belong.

1 factory office customer bank
2 engineer secretary doctor store
3 restaurant waiter nurse mechanic

3 *Groupwork*

Ask other people questions about their jobs.

What do you do?

Who do you work for?

I'm a. . .

For a big . . .

Vocabulary

4

What's the next word?

Example: Monday, Tuesday, ____
– Wednesday

1 eleven, twelve, thirteen, ____
2 ten, twenty, thirty, ____
3 January, February, ____
4 I work, she works, we ____
5 I know, you know, he ____

F Can you do it?

1 What about you?

a) Make questions and answer them.

Example: Can you use a word processor?
– Yes, I can./– No, I can't.

1   use a word processor

2   drive

3   play tennis

Ciao.
Au revoir.
Auf Wiedersehen.
Adiós.

5   speak Italian, French,
     German or Spanish

How
are
you
today?

Fine,
thanks.

6   answer easy questions
     in English

eighteen,
nineteen,
twenty,
twenty-one,
twenty-two,
. . .

7   count to one hundred in
     English

**b) Say two more things you
can do.**

I can play
tennis
and I can
ski, too.

12

4   ski

8   understand these words

c) Now say one more thing you can't do.

2 *Groupwork*

Ask other students what they can do.

3 *Writing*

How many sentences can you write?

I can	speak French
	use a computer
Can you	drive
	play tennis
I can't	do this exercise
	understand these words

Before you begin

1 You see a friend in the street. What do you say?

 a) How do you do?
 b) How are you?
 c) How?

2 Your friend is talking to a man. You don't know this man and your friend says, 'This is Jack Smith.' Jack says, 'How do you do?' What do you say?

 a) How do I do what?
 b) I'm fine, thanks.
 c) How do you do?

1

Read the conversation and complete the questions.

1 ____ is his name?
2 What ____ her name?
3 Where ____ they going?
4 ____ is she staying?
5 Is this ____ first visit?

• Now answer the questions.

2 *What about you?*

1 Are you staying in a hotel?
2 What are you doing now?
3 Where are you going after this lesson?
4 Is this your first lesson?
5 How do you say 'Is this your first visit?' in your language?

Listening

3

Listen to a different conversation. Then answer these questions.

1 Where is Tessa now?
2 What is the problem?
3 Is it really a problem?
4 How long is she staying?
5 What number do you hear?
6 Is it a telephone number?

Conversation

A young woman is at an international airport.
A young man is talking to her.

HE: Excuse me. Are you Tessa Saunders?
SHE: Yes, that's right.
HE: Good morning. My name is Alberto Ríos. I work for Mephisto Advertising.
SHE: Oh. How do you do?
HE: How do you do? Can I carry your bag?
SHE: No, that's all right, thank you. It isn't very heavy.
HE: A car is waiting for us. Please come this way.
SHE: Where are we going now?
HE: To your hotel.
SHE: Which hotel? Where am I staying?
HE: The Metropole.
SHE: Oh, yes. I think I know it.
HE: So this isn't your first . . . uh, how do you say in English . . . your first time here?
SHE: My first visit? No, it isn't.

Developing language

Grammar: questions

1

Look at Tessa's answers. What are the questions?

Example: 1 Tessa Saunders.
– What's your name?

1 Tessa Saunders.
2 S A U N D E R S.
3 At the Metropole Hotel.
4 For two nights.
5 From Liverpool.
6 No, I live in London now.
7 I work in an advertising agency.
8 No, I'm single. Why?

2

Make questions.

Example: Tessa from where is
– Where is Tessa from?

1 Tessa   married   is
2 you   married   are
3 Tessa   do   what   does
4 she   how long   staying   is
5 surname   her   what   is
6 you   this   exercise   do   can

- Now answer the questions.

 See Grammar Summary 2.2, page 78.

Vocabulary: greetings

3

Give the answers.

Example: 1 Hello.
– Hello.

1 Hello.
2 Good morning.
3 How do you do?
4 How are you?
5 Goodbye.

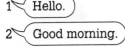

4

What are the words for the pictures?

Example: 1
– Good morning.

1
2
3
4

Vocabulary: opposites

5

Find the opposite.

Example: good
– bad

1 good   different
2 long   small
3 heavy   bad
4 same   late
5 hot   short
6 early   false
7 first   light
8 big   cold
9 true   last

Pronunciation: /iː/ she or /ɪ/ English

6

a) When is the sound different?

1 please she he England
2 she see he English
3 isn't English visit Japanese
4 international English we different
5 please me three English

b) Now listen and check.
c) Can you say these words, too?
   tea   easy   leave   live   listen   Italy

Can I help you?

1 What are you wearing now?
2 What do you usually wear at work or at school?
3 What size shoes do you wear?
4 What about the other things you are wearing?
   What size are they?

Conversation

A young man is in a department store in London.
His name is James Chen.

Salesman: Good afternoon. Can I help you, sir?
James: Yes, I'm looking for a suit.
Salesman: What size?
James: A thirty-eight jacket, I think, and thirty-two trousers.
Salesman: And what colour do you want, sir?
James: Dark grey or maybe dark blue. I'm not sure.
Salesman: Perhaps something like this?
James: Very nice. Um, how much is it?
Salesman: Only two hundred pounds.
James: Pardon? How much?
Salesman: Two hundred pounds, sir.
James: Oh! I'm afraid that's too much. I want . . . I mean, I'm looking for something that costs . . . uh . . . oh . . . about . . . uh.
Salesman: Yes? How much do you want to spend, sir?

1

Answer the questions.

1 Why is James in the department store?
2 What size is he?
3 What colour does he want?
4 Does he want to spend two hundred pounds?

Listening

2

Listen to the complete conversation. Then answer these questions.

1 How much can James spend?
2 The salesman shows him another suit. How much is it?
3 What is the suit made of?
4 Does James buy the blue suit?

3 *Roleplay*

A: You are a customer in a department store. Before you begin, think of these questions.
  • What do you want? Can you see it on the next page?
  • What colour do you want?
  • How much do you want to spend?
B: You work in the department store. Speak to the customer.

Useful language for A

• I'm looking for . . .
• Have you got a . . . in my size?

Useful language for B

• Can I help you?
• What size are you?
• What colour would you like?
• How much do you want to spend?

Exploring language

Grammar: personal pronouns and possessives

1

What's the missing word?

1 Where does ___ live?
2 What is ___ name?
3 Do you know ___?

4 Where does ___ live?
5 Do you know ___?
6 Do you know ___ name?

7 Do you know ___?
8 Where do ___ live?
9 What are ___ names?

2

Complete the table.

1	I	me	?
2	you	?	your
3	he	him	?
4	she	?	her
5	it	it	?
6	we	?	our
7	they	them	?

 See Grammar Summary 1, page 78.

Grammar: How much?/How many?

3

***How much* or *How many*?**

Example: ___ does that suit cost?
– How much

1 ___ bags are you taking with you?
2 ___ does this dictionary cost?
3 ___ students are there in your class?
4 ___ coffee do you want?
5 ___ cups of coffee do you want?

See Grammar Summary 6, page 80.

Vocabulary: clothes

4

Find the words for the pictures.

Example: 1
– dress

• shoes • hat • suit • dress • coat
• shirt and tie • trousers • boots • blouse

5

Study the definitions.

> **clothes** /kləʊðz/ things we wear; shirts, blouses, trousers, etc.
> **cloth** /klɒθ/ material we make clothes and other things with; cotton, wool, silk, etc.

Pronunciation: /əʊ/ clothes or /ɒ/ cloth

6

a) When is the sound different?

1 clothes nose knows cloth
2 cloth boss don't office
3 don't clothes go coffee
4 cloth cost office clothes

b) Now listen and check.

c) Say all the words with the /ɒ/ sound.
Then say all the words with the /əʊ/ sound.

Reading 🔊

Tessa Saunders works for Knight and Day. Knight and Day is an advertising agency with offices in London and New York.

Tessa lives in Wimbledon, a suburb of London. She usually gets up at six thirty. She goes to work on the Underground. It usually takes her about fifty minutes to get to her office. It's near Piccadilly Circus – about five minutes away on foot.

Tessa earns a good salary, but her job isn't easy. She usually starts work before nine in the morning and never finishes before seven or eight o'clock in the evening. Sometimes she leaves the office after nine or even ten o'clock. She often goes to bed after midnight and doesn't get very much sleep – perhaps five or six hours.

Tessa has a friend called Roger Mitchum. She doesn't see him very often. He lives in San Francisco. He works for a company that makes computer software.

1

Complete the questions.

Example: Where ——— Tessa live?
– does

1 Who ——— Tessa work for?
2 How long ——— it take her to get to work?
3 ——— she earn a good salary?
4 When ——— she usually start work?
5 ——— she usually leave the office early?
6 How much sleep ——— she usually get?
7 Where ——— her friend live?
8 What ——— he do?

• Now answer the questions.

2 *Groupwork*

There is a lot of information in the reading text about Tessa. Can you get the same information about people in your class?

When do you get up?

How do you get to work?

When do you start/finish work?

Developing language

Grammar: Present Simple

1

work or works?

1 Where do you ___?
2 I ___ for a big international company.
3 Where does Tessa ___?
4 She ___ for an advertising agency.
5 Does Roger ___ for an advertising agency, too?
6 No, he ___ for a company that makes software.
7 Do Donald Day and Richard Knight ___ in the same office?
8 No, they ___ in different offices.

2

Does or Do?

1 ___ you work for an advertising agency?
2 ___ Tessa like her work?
3 ___ you like your work?
4 ___ Roger earn a good salary?
5 ___ you want more money?
6 ___ Roger and Tessa live in the same city?

3

Make questions.

Example: live you do where
          – Where do you live?

1 you this understand do
2 English you do speak
3 Tessa in London live does
4 Roger in London too does live
5 a good salary earn do you
6 you to work get do how

4

Finish the next sentence.

Example: I earn a good salary. She . . .
          – earns a good salary.

1 She goes on the Underground. I . . .
2 She starts before nine. They . . .
3 Tessa understands this. We . . .
4 We go to work on the bus. My friend . . .
5 Tessa has got a good job. I . . .
6 She doesn't get much sleep. I . . .
7 I don't understand. He . . .

5

Make as many correct questions as you can.

1	2	3	4
What		Tessa	live
Where	*does*	you	get up
			earn
How much		Roger	cost
		they	get to work
How		this book	do work
When	*do*		go to bed
			have lunch

☞ See Grammar Summary 8, page 81.

Vocabulary: opposites

6

Find the opposite.

Example: start
          – finish

1	start	go to bed
2	easy	arrive
3	before	finish
4	never	come home
5	leave	far
6	here	difficult
7	get up	right
8	go to work	after
9	wrong	there
10	near	always

Pronunciation: /ɜ:/ her 📼

7

a) Is the sound the same or different?

1 w**or**k h**er**   6 l**ear**n **ear**n
2 w**or**d s**ir**   7 w**or**k l**ear**n
3 w**or**d w**or**k   8 f**or**ty w**or**k
4 sub**ur**b th**ir**teen 9 m**or**ning w**or**d
5 **ear**n w**or**ld

b) Now listen and check.

A problem

1 What is wrong with this conversation?

Why don't we have lunch sometime?

I don't know why. Tell me!

A   B

2 What is a good answer to A's question?

Conversation

Tessa is in her office. The phone rings.

TESSA: Hello?
DAVID: Hello, Tessa?
TESSA: Speaking.
DAVID: This is David Kale. Do you remember me?
TESSA: Hello, David? David Kale! Of course I remember you. How are you?
DAVID: Busy. Very busy. I've got a new job.
TESSA: A new job? You mean you don't work for . . . for . . . oh, I'm sorry. I always forget the name of that company.
DAVID: Orway. No, I don't work there any more. I'm with Artaud International now.
TESSA: The French company?
DAVID: Yes. Listen, I'd like to discuss something with you.
TESSA: Oh? What?
DAVID: A problem, but I don't want to talk about it now. Not on the phone, I mean. Why don't we meet for lunch sometime?
TESSA: Yes, of course. When?
DAVID: What about next Tuesday?
TESSA: That's the third, isn't it?
DAVID: Yes.
TESSA: Just a moment. Let me look in my diary.

1

Are these explanations right or wrong?

1 *Busy* means 'not working very much'.
2 *To forget* is the opposite of *to remember*.
3 People say *Of course* when they are very sure about something.
4 We say *I'd like to* . . . when we talk about things we want to do.
5 *Sometime* means 'at one time and at no other time'.
6 A *diary* tells you what time and what day it is.
7 When you say *Let me look in my diary*, you mean 'Just a moment. I'd like to look in my diary.'

2

Which four questions can you answer? Find two questions you can't answer.

1 Does Tessa remember David's name?
2 What name does she always forget?
3 Who does David work for now?
4 Why is he phoning?
5 What is his problem?
6 When can Tessa have lunch with him?

Listening

3

Listen to the complete conversation. Then answer these questions.

1 What day can Tessa and David meet?
2 At exactly what time?
3 Where?

Exploring language

Grammar: negatives

1

Read what Tessa says. What's different about you?

> 1 I come from Liverpool.
> 2 I live in Wimbledon.
> 3 I like classical music.
> 4 I speak two foreign languages.
> 5 I go to work on the Underground.
> 6 I work in an advertising agency.

- Say the same things if they are true about you. If they aren't true, say what is true.

Example:

> I come from Liverpool, too.

> I don't come from Liverpoool. I come from . . .

2

Make as many correct sentences as you can.

1	2	3	4
You I They We Tessa She Roger He This bus It	*don't* *doesn't*	live work go like know	in a bank in a city to London in London the answer your name beer Americans in America

3 *Writing*

Now use the table to write five or six negative sentences.

> ☞ See Grammar Summary 8.3, page 81.

Grammar: prepositions

4

from, of, to, on or *at*?

1 Richard Knight is the director ____ an advertising agency.
2 He's ____ the phone now.
3 Richard comes ____ Oxford, England.
4 He often goes ____ Los Angeles.
5 He's ____ the airport now.

> ☞ See Grammar Summary 3, page 79.

Vocabulary: see, hear and talk

5

Put the words below into the three groups.

Mouth 👄	Eyes 👀	Ears 👂
say		

- say • hear • see • listen to
- watch • look at • talk • speak

6

Now complete these sentences.

1 Do you often ____ the radio?
2 Do you often ____ television?
3 Hello. Pardon? I can't ____ you.
4 ____ the sun! Isn't it beautiful?
5 Look out of the window. What can you ____?
6 How many languages can you ____?
7 What's your problem? Do you want to ____ about it?
8 How do you ____ this word?

Pronunciation: /ɪ/ busy or /ʌ/ bus 📼

7

a) When is the sound different?

1 **i**s h**i**s b**u**sy disc**u**ss
2 **u**s b**u**s d**oe**s b**u**sy
3 c**o**lour y**ou**ng **u**p b**u**sy
4 b**u**sy v**i**sit s**u**burb l**i**sten

b) Now listen and check.

21

Monday morning

1

2

3

4

5

6

Reading 🔊

t's half past six on Monday morning. Tessa Saunders works in an advertising agency. She's having breakfast and reading a newspaper. The radio is on. She's listening to some music.

Richard Knight is Tessa's boss. He's having a shower.

It's half past seven and James Chen is putting on a new suit. James comes from Hong Kong, but he doesn't live there any more. He lives in London now and he has an interview for a job at ten o'clock this morning.

It's half past eight now. Richard Knight is driving to work. He isn't going very fast because the traffic is very heavy this morning.

It's half past nine now. Tessa is talking to Richard Knight. They're in his office. He's smoking a cigar.

James is talking to a policewoman. He's asking the way to Blake Street.

It's ten fifteen now. James Chen is in Tessa's office in Blake Street. She's interviewing him.

It's eleven o'clock now. James is waiting for a bus. It's cold and it's raining, but he's happy because he's got a job with Knight and Day.

1

Look at the pictures and read the text. Two pictures are missing. Which paragraphs in the text go with these missing pictures?

2

Look at the pictures with another student. Ask and answer questions.

Example: Picture 1
– Who is that?
– What is he doing?
– Where is he going?

Listening 🔊

3

Listen to the conversation. Then answer these questions.

1 Can you find two sentences in the reading text that go with the conversation?
2 Two people are talking. Who are they?
3 Where does one of them want to go?
4 What does the second person tell the first?

Developing language

Grammar: Present Simple/Progressive

1

Find answers (a–d) for the questions.

1 ◁ What do you do?

2 ◁ What are you doing?

3 ◁ Do you listen to the radio?

4 ◁ Are you listening to the radio?

a) I'm having breakfast.
b) Yes, why? Is it too loud?
c) Yes, usually in the morning.
d) I'm an engineer.

2

Look at picture 3 again on the opposite page. Then answer the questions below, like this: Yes/No/I don't know.

1 Is she reading a book?
2 Does she read books?
3 Does she drink wine?
4 Is she drinking wine?
5 Does she watch television?
6 Is she watching television?
7 Does she work?
8 Is she working?

3 *Groupwork*

Do people in your class do these things? Are they doing them now?

• watch television   • listen to the radio   • smoke
• go the cinema   •play football   • watch football
• read a newspaper   • drink wine

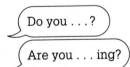

Do you . . . ?

Are you . . . ing?

Yes, I do./
No, I don't.

Yes, I am./
No, I'm not.

☞ See Grammar Summary 8–9, page 81.

Vocabulary: opposites

4

Find the opposite.

Example: up
– down

sad far off
poor slow late
right cool down
young/new

up fast on old
left near early
warm happy rich

Vocabulary: directions

5

Tell someone how to get to these places.

• the restaurant **R**   • the post office **PO**
• the bank **B**   • the hotel **H**   • the station **S**
• the car park **CP**

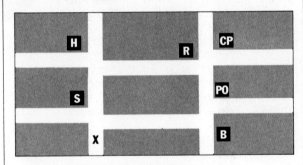

X = *you and the tourist*

Useful language
• Excuse me. Can you tell me the way to . . . ?
• Go straight ahead.
• Take the first/second turning on the right/left.
• Then turn first/second right/left.
• Go past the . . .
• The . . . is on the right/left.

Pronunciation: *thirteen* or *thirty* 📼

6

Listen. Which number do you hear? Is it from group A or group B?

A	B
□ ☐	☐ □
thirteen	thirty
13 14 15 16	30 40 50 60
17 18 19	70 80 90

The interview

Conversation

Tessa Saunders is interviewing James Chen. Here is part of the interview.

TESSA: Yes, that's very interesting. Now, James, tell me something about yourself.

JAMES: Well, as you can see from my application, I was born in Hong Kong but I've got a British passport. I'm twenty-three years old, I speak three languages and I've got a Certificate in Advertising Studies.

TESSA: And you're interested in a career in advertising.

JAMES: Yes, I am. Very interested.

TESSA: Why?

JAMES: Well, uh . . . I like working with words and ideas. And I like meeting people, too. And . . . uh . . . well . . .

TESSA: . . . Right . . . now . . . let's turn to some other skills. . . . Tell me. Can you type?

JAMES: Yes, but not very fast. Why? Is typing necessary for the job?

TESSA: No, not really. But it always helps if you can use a wordprocessor or a computer.

JAMES: Yes, of course. I think I can do that.

TESSA: Well, now. Have you got any questions? I mean, is there anything you'd like to ask me?

JAMES: Yes, can you tell me a little more about the job, please?

TESSA: Yes, of course . . .

1

Complete the questions.

1 How old ____ James?
2 How many languages ____ he speak?
3 Where ____ he born?
4 Why ____ he interested in advertising?
5 ____ he type?
6 ____ he got any questions?

• Now answer the questions.

2 *What about you?*

1 Where were you born?
2 How many languages do you speak?
3 Can you type very fast?
4 What are you interested in?

3 *Groupwork*

Which jobs are people in your class interested in? Why are they interested?

Trainee Managers
Good at maths? Want to earn a good salary? Good opportunity to start in supermarket management.
Write to:

Alan Kirk Open Gate Stores,
187, Ashley Cross,
POOLE, Dorset, BH14 10NS.

Butcher's Apprentice
Hard work but good pay. Free meat and sausage.
Phone Bill, 721773.

Hotel Receptionist
Chance for intelligent young person to learn hotel business. 3 pm to 11 pm, six days a week. Apply to: The Manager, Queen's Hotel, Horsham.

4 *Roleplay*

A: Interview B for the job he/she wants. Ask questions.

• How old . . . ?
• Have you got a . . . ?

Think of more questions.

B: Answer A's questions.

Exploring language

Grammar: *has/have got*

1

Look at what the dictionary says. Then answer the questions.

> **have** (also **have got** *Br E*) to possess; own:
> *She has blue eyes. Have you got a pencil?*
> *Do you have a pencil? This coat has no pockets.*
> *He's got a bad cold.*

1 There is a difference here between British English and American English. What is it?
2 Look at the last example (*He's got a bad cold*). What does *'s* mean here? Is it the short form of the word *is* or the word *has*?
3 Which statements below do you think are true?
   a) In British English we can say, 'I *have* a driving licence' or 'I*'ve got* a driving licence.'
   b) You can say both in American English, too.
   c) Americans often say, 'I *don't have* a licence.'
   d) British people don't understand Americans when they say this.
   e) British people usually say, 'I *haven't got* a licence.'
   f) The word *got* in *have got* or *has got* isn't really necessary, but British people often use it.

2

What are the missing words?

1 Excuse me, ____ you got the time?
2 I'm sorry but I haven't ____ my watch.
3 Tessa Saunders ____ got a good job.
4 This advertising agency ____ got an office in New York and one in London, too.
5 Both my wife and I ____ got colds.
6 How many children ____ you got?

● Look at sentences 1 and 6 again. How do you think most Americans ask these questions?

3 *Groupwork*

Find out how many people in your class have got these things.

● a car ● a dictionary ● a camera ● a good job
● a brother or a sister ● more than two brothers or sisters ● a credit card ● more than one credit card

4 *Writing*

Write down eight sentences about what people in your class have got and haven't got.

Example:

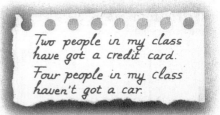

> *Two people in my class have got a credit card.*
> *Four people in my class haven't got a car.*

5

Give the full form of the words in *italics*. Is it *is* or *has*?

Example: What*'s* Tessa doing?
   – is

1 It*'s* late.   3 She*'s* got a good job.
2 She*'s* English.   4 He*'s* got blue eyes.

● What is the full word in these sentences?

1 You*'re* the boss.
2 I*'ve* got it.

> See Grammar Summary 11, page 82.

Vocabulary: money

6

Find a word that has nothing to do with money.

1 dollar   mark   tea   yen
2 money   dinner   cash   cheque
3 salary   pay   tip   lunch
4 snack   earn   spend   cost
5 cheap   expensive   breakfast   price

Pronunciation: /θ/ th*ink*

7

a) Say these words.

	A	B
1	three	tree
2	think	sink
3	thing	sing
4	both	boat

b) Now listen. Which word do you hear? Is it from group A or group B?

Two people, two jobs

Are there people in your class who do these things?

- travel to foreign countries
- use English at work
- work very late

Reading 📼

Roger and Tessa are friends, but she never sees him any more because he lives in San Francisco. He works for a software company there. He earns a very good salary.

Roger often travels to countries in Asia and South and Central America, but never to Europe.

'In the future, we hope to sell more of our software in Europe. But at the moment I have no reason to travel there,' he says.

When Roger is in San Franciso, he usually gets to his office at 8.30am and leaves around 5.30pm. His weekends are usually free.

Tessa's job with an advertising agency in London is interesting, but she works very long hours. She often leaves the office at eight or nine in the evening and often works at weekends, as well.

She sometimes travels to Spain and Italy.

'I go there to discuss plans with clients. But my agency also has clients in Germany, France and Greece. I hope to travel there in the future too,' she says.

1

Discuss these words and meanings.

1 What is the difference between these words?
  a) salary b) wages c) tips
2 Which word here is different from the others?
  never often always usually
3 Which person do you think has *clients*?
  - a doctor - a waiter - a policeman
  - an architect or lawyer
4 You tell your boss you want more money. Your boss says, 'Give me your *reasons*.' What do you do?
  a) say nothing more
  b) say why you want more money
  c) say, 'Thank you very much', and leave
5 There are four examples of the word *there* in the text. Does it always mean the same thing?

2

Talk about these things.

- Roger's job
- his company's plans or hopes for the future
- the reason he doesn't see Tessa any more
- some of the differences between Tessa's job and Roger's job

3 *What about you?*

Talk about things you hope to do in the future.

> Someday I hope I can . . .

> Someday I'd like to . . .

Developing language

Grammar: frequency adverbs

1

Read about Tessa.

1 I never go to bed before eleven.
2 I always get up before seven.
3 I usually have only toast and tea for breakfast.
4 I often have lunch in a restaurant.
5 I sometimes drink champagne.
6 I rarely eat meat.

- Add these words to the chart below.

rarely   often   sometimes   never

1 always	●●●●●●●
2 usually	●●● ●●●
3 ?	● ●●● ●
4 ?	● ●
5 ?	●
6 ?	

2 *What about you?*

How often do you do these things? Sometimes? Never? Often? Or rarely?

Example: eat in restaurants
– I sometimes eat in restaurants./
I never eat in restaurants.

1 listen to the radio in the morning
2 listen to the radio at work
3 buy expensive clothes
4 go to the cinema
5 play football
6 watch football
7 drink beer or wine
8 eat foreign food
9 work on Sundays

3 *Groupwork*

Tell someone in your class what you often do. Then find out how often they do it.

I often go to bed after midnight. What about you?

I sometimes go to bed after midnight, but not very often.

See Grammar Summary 13, page 82.

Vocabulary: customers and services

4

Find the connection.

Example: passenger
– plane, bus, train, ship

1 passenger   doctor, hospital
2 customer   lawyer, agency
3 guest   hotel
4 patient   plane, bus, train, ship
5 client   shop, department store

5

Where do these people work?

Example: nurse
– hospital

1 secretary   3 receptionist   5 mechanic
2 pilot   4 salesperson   6 engineer

Pronunciation: /ʃ/ shop or /tʃ/ chop

6

a) Can you say these words?

shop   chop   wash   watch

b) Now say these words. Which ones have a /ʃ/ sound in them? Which ones have a /tʃ/ sound?

1 finish   shoes   cash
2 cheque   cheap   catch
3 information   patient   machine
4 China   which   future
5 application   champagne   international
6 picture   butcher   natural

c) Listen and check.

What do you suggest?

1 Talk about the food you like.
2 Talk about the food you don't like.

Conversation

Roger Mitchum is in Tokyo. He is talking to his company's distributor in Japan, Mr Yamada.

YAMADA: The software's very good. Our customers like the new software. Sales are increasing.
ROGER: I'm glad to hear that.
YAMADA: But there are some problems.
ROGER: Oh, what kind of problems?
YAMADA: I'd like to explain them later. Perhaps we can discuss them at dinner this evening?
ROGER: Yes, of course.
YAMADA: By the way, where would you like to go this evening? I mean, what kind of food would you like to eat?
ROGER: Well, I'm not sure. What do you suggest?
YAMADA: What about sashimi? Would you like that?
ROGER: Sashimi? What's that? I'm afraid I don't know very much about Japanese food.
YAMADA: It's raw fish or raw seafood. It's very good!
ROGER: Uh huh. I'd like to try that some other time perhaps. Can you suggest something else?
YAMADA: Yes, of course.

1

Are these explanations right or wrong?

1 When a number *increases*, it goes up.
2 When you *suggest* something, you are saying 'this is the one and only thing we can do'.
3 Food is *raw* after you cook it, not before.
4 *Something else* means 'something more' or 'something different'.

2

Complete the questions.

1 ___ the customers like the new software?
2 ___ sales increasing?
3 ___ Roger know very much about Japanese food?
4 What ___ sashimi?
5 ___ Roger like to eat sashimi this evening?

• Now ask someone else the complete questions.

Listening

3

Look at the menu and listen.

Seafood Cocktail
Fresh Fruit Cocktail

Grilled Lamb Chops
Fillet Steak
Barbecued Chicken
Pacific Salmon

Fresh Salad
Vegetables of the Day

Potatoes   Rice

1 What does Roger order?
2 What does Mr Yamada order?
3 What is the problem?

Exploring language

Grammar: *I like/I'd like*

1

What's the difference?

1 I like a glass of red wine.

2 I'd like a glass of red wine.

3 I like going to the cinema.

4 I'd like to go to the cinema.

- Find sentences above that mean these things.

a) There's a film on at the cinema. I want to see it.
b) I often go to the cinema. I like it.
c) I am not saying I want a glass of red wine now. I am telling you that I drink a glass of red wine sometimes and that I like it.
d) Please bring me a glass of red wine.

2

***Do you like* or *Would you like*?**

1 ____ some coffee now or later?
2 ____ to go to a Japanese restaurant this evening?
3 ____ sleeping late on Sundays or do you usually get up early?
4 ____ some more food?
5 ____ coffee or tea for breakfast? I mean, what do you usually have?
6 ____ coffee or tea for breakfast this morning?
7 ____ to be very rich and famous?

Would you like the bill now or later, sir?

3 *Groupwork*

Find out what people in your class like doing at the weekend.

Useful language

- What *do* you *like doing* at the weekend?
- I *like going* to the cinema/*reading*/*walking*.

Now find out what they would like to do this weekend.

Useful language

- What *would* you *like to do* this weekend?
- I think I'*d like to go* to the cinema/*see* a film.

☞ See Grammar Summary 14, page 82.

Vocabulary: food

4

Find the word that doesn't belong.

1 meat   vegetables   glass   fruit
2 peas   beef   pork   lamb
3 beans   potatoes   carrots   fish
4 fried   raw   boiled   grilled
5 salt   sugar   chicken   pepper
6 knife   fork   spoon   rice

5

Put more words into these groups.

Meat	Fish	Vegetables	Fruit
beef	salmon	beans	oranges

Pronunciation /uː/ fo**o**d or /ʊ/ f**oo**t

6

a) When is the sound different?

1 w**ou**ld   g**oo**d   c**oo**k   f**oo**d
2 f**oo**d   f**oo**t   t**oo**   sp**oo**n
3 f**oo**t   p**u**t   w**ou**ld   n**oo**n
4 b**oo**k   c**oo**k   l**oo**k   sp**oo**n

b) Now listen and check.

5   Two companies

Reading

Manfred Kernholz
Marketing Director, T.R.S.

Nathalie Artaud
Director, Artaud International

T.R.S. is a large German company in the electronics business. The main office and factory are located near Munich, in Germany. The company employs over four thousand people.

The company began in 1908. At that time they made telephones, but now they manufacture television sets, stereos and computers, as well.

T.R.S. is now developing a new video camera. The company plans to sell it next year.

Artaud International is a medium-sized company, with about four hundred employees. The main office is located in Paris, but the factory is in Amboise, about 200 kilometres away.

The company began in 1947. At that time it manufactured shoes, but it now makes sportswear, as well. The company plans to sell more of its products in Britain and the United States. Sales are not very good there at the moment.

Before you begin

1 How many of these company names do you know?
   • Boeing   • Cardin   • Sony   • Olivetti
   • Mercedes   • Leica
2 What do they make?
3 Give some more names of companies. Talk about what they make.

1

Find the words or phrases in the text that mean these things.

1 gives work to
2 where you find managers and the General Director
3 people who work for someone
4 make something with machines
5 design, plan and begin making something
6 now

2

Make questions about the two companies using these words. Discuss the answers, too.

• What . . . ?
• Where . . . ?
• How many . . . ?
• When . . . ?

Developing language

Grammar: past, present and future

1

What's the connection?

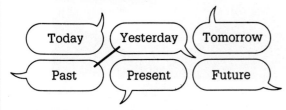

- *Past* goes with *Yesterday*. What do the other words go with?

- Now answer these questions.

1 What day is it today?
2 What day was it yesterday?
3 What day will it be tomorrow?

2

Past, present or future?

Example: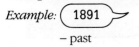

– past

- What about these words and dates?

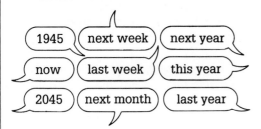

3

Are these sentences about the present or the past?

Example: It's cold.
– present

1 It was cold.
2 We were cold and hungry.
3 We're cold and hungry.
4 I like it.
5 I liked it.
6 Did you like it, too?
7 Do you like it, too?
8 It's beginning to rain.
9 It began to rain.

4

Study the examples. What's the difference in form?

	Present	Past
1	I work for T.R.S.	I work*ed* for T.R.S.
2	She works there.	She work*ed* there.
3	I like it.	I lik*ed* it.
4	She likes it.	She lik*ed* it.

5

These sentences are not true in the present, but they are true in the past. Make them true.

Example: Romeo loves Juliet.
– Romeo loved Juliet.

1 Juliet loves Romeo very much.
2 Marilyn Monroe lives in Beverly Hills.
3 James Dean lives in New York.
4 She likes reading books.
5 He likes driving fast cars.

6 *Writing*

What's the past form?

Example: starts
– started

1 start	4 types	7 phone
2 listen	5 type	8 discuss
3 listens	6 hope	9 watches

- Now write five sentences in the past about yourself.

 See Grammar Summary 15, page 83.

Vocabulary: time

7

Find the word that doesn't belong.

1 yesterday   last year   past   now
2 today   now   at the moment   yesterday
3 yesterday   last week   this week   last month
4 often   never   usually   in the past
5 soon   in the future   next Friday   last Sunday
6 tomorrow   next year   in a few minutes   rarely

No alternative

Conversation

Tessa's boss, Richard Knight, is in his office. A client in Munich, Manfred Kernholz, is phoning him.

RICHARD: Hello, Herr Kernholz. How are you?
KERNHOLZ: Very well. And you?
RICHARD: Just fine. What can I do for you?
KERNHOLZ: It's about the date of our next meeting.
RICHARD: The date of our next meeting?
KERNHOLZ: Yes, when I was in London at the end of last month, we wanted to discuss a number of things. But we didn't discuss all of them. There wasn't enough time. That's why we planned another meeting for the eleventh of this month. Perhaps you remember.
RICHARD: Of course I remember, Herr Kernholz. Is there a problem with the date?
KERNHOLZ: Yes, that's the reason I'm phoning now. I'm afraid the eleventh is no longer very convenient for us.
RICHARD: Oh, I see. Hmm.
KERNHOLZ: Is it possible to meet on the fourth instead?
RICHARD: On the fourth? Oh, so soon?
KERNHOLZ: Yes. I'm terribly sorry. I really didn't want to change things like this, but I'm afraid there's no alternative.

1
Do you agree with these explanations?

1 When people say *There isn't enough time*, they mean 'the time is too short'.
2 *Convenient* means 'difficult to do'.
3 *There's no alternative* means 'this is the only thing we can do'.

2
Discuss the questions.

1 When was Kernholz in London?
2 Why was he there?
3 Why did he and Richard plan another meeting?
4 When did they want to meet again?
5 Why is Kernholz phoning now?

Listening

3
Listen to the complete conversation. Then answer these questions.

1 What's the problem?
2 What's the reason for the problem?
3 What does Richard suggest?
4 What does Kernholz think of the idea?

Exploring language

Grammar: was/were

1

Is the small change in one word important? Is it only a small change in the meaning, too?

1 My boss *is* a nice man.
   My boss *was* a nice man.
2 My mother's eyes *are* blue.
   My mother's eyes *were* blue.

2

These sentences are correct in one way, but not in another way. Can you do something so that they are correct in both ways?

Example: Marilyn Monroe is an actress.
       – Marilyn Monroe was an actress.

1 She is married to a baseball player.
2 Ronald Reagan is the President of the United States.
3 Romeo and Juliet are Italian.
4 You are a complete beginner in English.
5 Japanese cars are very small and they aren't very good.
6 Victoria is the Queen of England.

3

Make these sentences into good questions.

Example: Kernholz was here . . . let's see . . . when?
       – When was Kernholz here?

1 He was here . . . let's see . . . how long ago?
2 The people with him were . . . uh . . . who?
3 They discussed . . . uh . . . let's see . . . what?
4 They had lunch . . . hmm . . . where?
5 Yesterday evening you were . . . where?
6 You did . . . what?

 See Grammar Summary 16, page 83.

Vocabulary: numbers

4

Which number is different from the others?

1 one two third four

2 five six seven eighth

3 nine tenth eleventh twelfth

5 *Roleplay*

Look at this lift sign from a building in London.

7	FAR HORIZONS VIDEO
6	CITY FINANCIAL SERVICES
5	EAST-WEST EXPORT
4	WEST-EAST IMPORT
3	JOLLY CLEAN
2	BELL AND WINTER ADVERTISING
1	ACE PRIVATE DETECTIVE AGENCY
G	RECEPTION

A: You work in the building in London. People often ask you this question. Give the answers.

Excuse me. Can you tell me what floor (Far Horizons Video) is on?

Yes, it's on the (seventh) floor.

B: Think of all the possible questions people can ask A about the companies in the building. They want to know what floor certain companies are on.

Pronunciation: present or past

6

Listen to these sentences. Which one do you hear? Is it from group A or group B?

	A	**B**
1	Are you there?	Were you there?
2	I work all day.	I worked all day.
3	They live here.	They lived here.
4	They like it.	They liked it.

6 Yesterday

Reading 🔊

Tessa got up at six thirty yesterday morning. She didn't feel very well, but she went to work all the same.

She went to work on the Underground and got to her office at eight o'clock. At half past nine, she had a meeting with her boss, Richard Knight, and at ten o'clock she interviewed a young man, James Chen, for a job. Tessa liked him very much and he got the job.

She didn't have very much time for lunch. She was too busy, and she wasn't very hungry anyway, so she had a sandwich and a cup of coffee in a small café near the office. At two o'clock she had a meeting with a photographer.

She didn't like one of his photographs at all. She thought it was all wrong for the advertisement they were planning. They argued about it, but finally he agreed with her.

She left the office around eight yesterday evening. She got home about nine and had dinner alone. Then she watched television for a few minutes, but she didn't like the programme, so she turned it off. She went to bed at half past ten. That's very early for her. She usually goes to bed much later.

1

We can't ask these questions about yesterday. What are the questions we can ask?

1 When does she get up?
2 How does she feel when she gets up?
3 What does she do then?
4 What does she do before lunch?
5 How much time does she have for lunch?
6 What does she do after lunch?
7 When does she get home?
8 Does she have dinner alone?
9 What does she do after dinner?

• Now answer the correct questions.

2 *Groupwork*

Ask other people about their day yesterday.

> When did you . . . ? I got up at . . .
>
> Where did you . . . ? I had lunch in . . .
>
> How did you . . . ? I went to . . . by . . .

Developing language

Grammar: regular and irregular past

1

Look at the verb forms below. Which are regular? Which are irregular?

1 I worked . . .	5 She came . . .
2 I watched . . .	6 They had . . .
3 We discussed . . .	7 He took . . .
4 They argued . . .	8 I saw . . .

2

Look at the verbs in column A. Can you put the past form in column B?

	A (present)	B (past)
1	live/lives	lived
2	finish/finishes	?
3	explain/explains	?
4	like/likes	?
5	go/goes	?
6	think/thinks	?
7	get/gets	?
8	have/has	?
9	leave/leaves	?

3

Roger did these things yesterday. Talk about what you did.

Example: 1 – I wasn't in Tokyo. I was in Madrid./
I was in Tokyo, too.

> 1 I was in Tokyo yesterday.
> 2 I woke up at six fifteen.
> 3 I had breakfast in my hotel.
> 4 I spent the morning with some businessmen.
> 5 In the afternoon I went shopping.
> 6 At ten p.m. yesterday evening I was in a plane over the Pacific Ocean.
> 7 I had steak for dinner and drank some red wine with it.

☞ See Grammar Summary 16, pages 83–84.

Vocabulary: *have*

4

How many different meanings of *have* can you find here?

1 What do you usually have for breakfast?
2 Do you have a shower every morning?
3 I always have coffee in the morning.
4 Roger had a sports car last year.
5 I had a letter from Tessa yesterday.
6 My sister had a baby last week.

- In which sentence above does *have* mean

a) get   b) drink   c) eat
d) possess/own   e) none of these things

5

Can you use *have* in all these sentences?

1 Let's _____ a party next weekend.
2 What did you _____ for lunch?
3 We _____ a test every month.
4 Did you _____ a good time at the party?
5 I usually _____ the bus to work.
6 Please _____ some eggs for me at the shop.
7 Did you _____ a good day at work?

Pronunciation: stress

6

a) Say the words below. Which part of the word is the stressed part?

☐ ☐	☐ ☐
thir-ty	thir-**teen**
ar-gue	dis-**cuss**
an-swer	su-**ggest**

b) Now say these words. Which are like thirty? Which are like thirteen?

enjoy	modern	coffee
employ	question	inform
explain	hotel	problem
discuss	client	moment
doctor	patient	programme
airport	shopping	music

c) Now listen and repeat.

d) Talk about these questions.

1 What are the words here that look like words in your own language?
2 Is the stress the same or different?

Plans

1 Which of these things can you plan?
  • the weather
  • travel
  • a party
2 Have you got any plans? What are they?

Conversation

Tessa's boss, Richard Knight, wants to talk to her.

RICHARD: Now, Manfred Kernholz phoned earlier this morning.
TESSA: Pardon? Who?
RICHARD: Manfred Kernholz from T.R.S. in Munich. He was here at the beginning of the year. Don't you remember?
TESSA: From Munich? Oh, yes. He was the tall man, wasn't he? With fair hair?
RICHARD: No, that was Hans Landau, his assistant. Kernholz is older than Landau. And his hair is darker. He's the Marketing Director. Landau's only his assistant.
TESSA: Oh . . . well . . . what about him?
RICHARD: He wants to have a meeting next week. Can you go?
TESSA: Where? To Munich?
RICHARD: Yes. That's what I said.
TESSA: When?
RICHARD: Just a moment ago. I said . . .
TESSA: No, I meant the meeting, Richard. When is it?
RICHARD: Oh. On the fourth.
TESSA: The fourth?
RICHARD: Yes. What's wrong? Did you have other plans for that day?
TESSA: Yes. I wanted to have lunch with David Kale then.
RICHARD: Who's he?
TESSA: He works for Artaud International.
RICHARD: This is more important, Tessa. Can't you have lunch with . . . uh . . . what's his name . . . some other time?
TESSA: I think so, but I'm not sure.

1

Answer the questions.

1 Who is Manfred Kernholz?
2 Who was with him in London?
3 Describe the two men.
4 Why is Richard talking about him now?
5 When and where is the meeting?
6 What's Tessa's problem?

Listening

2

Listen to the complete conversation. Then look at these sentences. Which are true and which are false?

1 The meeting in Munich is about a new British video camera.
2 They hope to sell a hundred or a thousand cameras in Britain in a year.
3 Richard says *sorry* because he doesn't remember what Landau said at the beginning of the meeting.

4 March

Meet David Kale for lunch.

Exploring language

Grammar: comparatives

1

Look at the two women and answer the questions.

Nathalie Artaud
Director
Artaud International

Tessa Saunders
Account executive
Knight and Day
Advertising

1 Who do you think is younger?
2 Who do you think is older?
3 Who do you think earns more money?
4 Which of the two do you think has a more important job?
5 Who has shorter hair?

2

What's the other word in the pair?

1	good	better	
2	bad	?	
3	?	older	
4	young	?	
5	?	more important	
6	expensive	?	
7	?	more interesting	
8	intelligent	?	
9	small	?	
10	difficult	?	

☞ See Grammar Summary 18, pages 84–85.

Grammar: think

3

What word is missing in the two answers?

> Can you come to the meeting?

> Yes, I think . . .

> No, I don't think . . .

- Answer these questions. Say what you think. Here is another answer.

> I have no idea.

1 Is English an important language?
2 Is it a very difficult language to learn?
3 Is it more difficult than German?
4 Is English a more useful language in international business than Japanese?
5 Is a Mercedes more expensive than a Ford?

Vocabulary: 'in between' words

4

What's the 'in between' word? Here are some of the missing words. Where do they go?

- middle-aged   • of medium height
- warm/cool   • centre

1	small	medium	large
2	beginning	?	end
3	young	?	old
4	left	?	right
5	breakfast	?	dinner
6	cold	?	hot
7	short	?	tall

Pronunciation: stress 📼

5

a) Say the words. Which syllable is stressed?

☐ ☐ ☐
Example: – be-gi-nning

1 un-der-stand
2 ex-pen-sive
3 te-le-phone
4 im-por-tant
5 mar-ket-ing
6 di-ffi-cult
7 com-pa-ny
8 a-ssis-tant

b) Now listen and repeat.

7 When do you want to go?

Before you begin

1 How do you say these times in English?
   • 3.15   • 3.45   • 13.10   •15.40
2 How do you say these dates?
   • 10 Nov, 1926   • 24.9.96   • your date of birth
3 You are getting information on the telephone. The person you are speaking to says, 'Can you hold?' What do you do?
   a) Wait.
   b) Ask, 'Hold what?'
   c) Say, 'All right. Give it to me.'

Conversation 📼

Tessa's secretary is phoning a travel agency.

CLERK: Hello. Can I help you?
PENNY: Oh, good morning. My name is Penny Miles, from Knight and Day Advertising. I'd like some information about flights to Munich, please.
CLERK: When do you want to go there?
PENNY: I'm not going. My boss is. And she wants to leave on the fourth.
CLERK: At what time of day?
PENNY: As early as possible.
CLERK: Can you hold for a moment?
PENNY: Yes. . .
CLERK: . . . Let's see. There's a British Airways flight from London Heathrow at eight fifteen.
PENNY: Quarter past eight. I see. And there's nothing earlier than that?
CLERK: No, that's the first flight.
PENNY: I see. When does it arrive?
CLERK: At eleven am.
PENNY: Eleven o'clock exactly?
CLERK: Yes.
PENNY: It's an hour later in Munich than it is here, isn't it?
CLERK: Uh . . . I think so. Let me see. Yes.

1

Make questions.

Example: when Tessa leave want to does
   – When does Tessa want to leave?

1 where go want to does she
2 when first flight is the
3 what time arrive in Munich does it
4 in Munich is it than in London
   earlier or later

• Now answer the questions

Listening 📼

2

Listen and then answer these questions.

1 A woman is speaking. Where do you think she is?
2 Who is she speaking to?
3 Where are the people going?
4 Who is the first part of the message for?
5 What are the numbers you hear in the second part of the message?
6 Your number is 42K. What do you do?

Developing language

Grammar: *as/than*

1

Study the examples.

1 Is it the same time in Munich *as* it is in London?
2 No, it's one hour later there *than* it is here.
3 Do you think Tessa earns *as* much *as* her boss?
4 Do you think he earns more *than* she does?

2 *What about you?*

Complete the questions.

1 Do you earn ___ much ___ your boss?
2 Would you like to earn more ___ you earn now?
3 Would you like to travel more or less ___ you do now?
4 Do you think that your English is better or worse ___ it was last month?

• Discuss the answers.

3

Do you usually do these things earlier or later than Tessa or at the same time?

Example: She usually gets up at six thirty.

> I usually get up earlier than that.

> I always get up later than that.

> I get up at the same time.

1 Tessa usually has breakfast at seven.
2 She leaves for work at seven forty.
3 She starts work at eight thirty.

4 She usually has lunch at twelve thirty.
5 She often goes home at eight or even nine in the evening.
6 She often has dinner very late – sometimes at ten o'clock.
7 She never goes to bed before midnight.
8 She usually gets about six hours sleep.

> See Grammar Summary 18.5, page 85.

Vocabulary: leaving and arriving

4

Can you put these words in two groups?

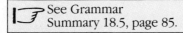

1 starting a journey

2 finishing a journey

• go   • arrive   • get to
• land   • come   • depart
• leave   • take off

1 Which of these words can we use only for planes?
2 Which words can we use for trains, buses or ships?

5

What's the missing word?

Example: Tessa goes ___ work every morning.
  – to

1 Flight BA 950 departs ___ London at a quarter past eight and arrives ___ Munich one hour and forty-five minutes later.
2 Where do you come ___ ?
3 Ladies and gentlemen. We are now landing ___ London Heathrow Airport.
4 Does this bus go ___ the airport?
5 Does it stop ___ the station, too?
6 Can you tell me when we get ___ Piccadilly Circus, please?

Pronunciation: /h/ here

6

a) Is the sound of the words the same or different?

1 here	hear	5 and	hand
2 ear	hear	6 at	hat
3 air	hair	7 our	hour
4 old	hold	8 eat	heat

b) Listen and check.

c) Now say these words. When is the sound different?

hear   hand   hair   hour

Advice column

Before you begin

1 Are the man and woman arguing about their friends or discussing them?

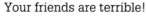

Your friends are terrible!

Yes, they are. I don't like any of them.

No, they aren't!

Well, I don't like some of your friends, either.

2 What do you have arguments about?

Reading

These two letters appeared in an English magazine.

> " I have a very good job, but I think my life was better before I got it.
>
> I often went to the theatre before. I saw some good films, and I went to parties, too. Now I don't do any of those things.
>
> Now I go to work very early and I come home very late, too. I had some very good friends before, but I don't see any of them now.
>
> When I come home, I always feel very tired. I don't even watch television or listen to the radio any more. I eat and then I go to bed.
>
> Do you think there is something wrong with me? "

Peter T. Bristol

> " I have a better job than my boyfriend and earn more than he does. I don't think this is important, but he often talks about it.
>
> We often have arguments about this and other things. For example, he doesn't like any of my friends. But when I say that I don't like some of his friends either, he gets very angry.
>
> I don't want to see him any more, but he says that he doesn't want to lose me and that he can't live without me.
>
> What can I do? "

Loretta S. Birmingham

1

Do you agree with the explanations?

1 *I had some good friends before* means 'I haven't got these friends now'.
2 *I saw some good films* and 'I see some good films' mean the same thing.
3 People are often *tired* at the end of the day.
4 When people have *arguments*, they never get angry.
5 When you *lose* something, you had it before but you haven't got it any more.

2

Answer the questions.

1 Is Peter very happy in his new job?
2 What was better before? What is worse now?
3 What do Loretta and her boyfriend argue about?
4 Why doesn't she leave her boyfriend?

3 *What about you?*

Are there things you did before that you don't do any more? Talk about them.

Example:

When I was younger, I often went to the cinema. I played the guitar, too. I don't do that any more.

Exploring language

Grammar: *some/any*

1

Discuss the difference.

1. I don't like *some* of your friends.
2. I don't like *any* of your friends.
3. I don't know *some* of the people here.
4. I don't know *any* of the people here.

- Find sentences above that mean these things.

a) There are a number of people (I'm not saying how many) that I don't know.
b) There is not one person here that I know.
c) I think all your friends are terrible.
d) Not all your friends but two or three (perhaps more) are terrible.

2

Complete the sentences with *some* or *any*. You can use either *some* or *any* in one of them. Which one?

1. I don't want ____ food. I couldn't eat a thing!
2. There are ____ words here that I don't understand.
3. I can't understand ____ of these words here. Not one of them!
4. Have you got ____ money?
5. I haven't got ____ money at all. Look! My pockets are empty.
6. Could you give me ____ money? I don't need much.
7. There are ____ people in the next room. I can hear them.
8. The room was empty when I looked in. There weren't ____ people there at all.
9. I understand most of the words here, but there are still ____ that I don't understand.

📖 See Grammar Summary 12, page 82.

Vocabulary: *see*

3

Here are some of the important meanings of *see*.

1. Look over there! What can you see?
2. I'm sorry but I can't see you today.
3. See a doctor as soon as you can.
4. I can't come on Monday. | I see. What about Tuesday?

- Find the example in which *see* means
a) go to   b) understand   c) meet, talk to

4

You can use *see* in most of these sentences. But in two of them you can't. Which two?

1. The director can ____ you at three o'clock.
2. I really can't ____ how I can help. I'm sorry.
3. A: Now do you understand?
   B: Yes, I think I ____ now. Thank you.
4. How often do you ____ your brother?
5. Would you like to ____ that film?
6. How often do you ____ television?
7. ____ these mistakes! They're terrible!
8. Please turn on the light. I can't ____ anything!

Pronunciation: /æ/ bad or /e/ bed 📼

5

a) Say these words.

man   men   Annie   any

b) Now say these words. Which have the sound of /æ/ in *bad*? Which have the sound of /e/ in *bed*?

1. than   then   and   end
2. had   bad   head   bed
3. said   says   send   friend

c) Listen and check.

When they were younger

1 Where were you born?
2 Did you grow up there, too?
3 How old were you when you had your first English lesson?
4 Talk about yourself when you were younger. For example, what subjects did you study at school? Which ones did you like?

Reading 🔊

Tessa was born in Liverpool. She went to school and grew up there.

Roger Mitchum was born in London, but he didn't grow up or go to school there. His father got a job in San Francisco when Roger was four, and the whole family went there.

Roger came back to England when he was eighteen. He met Tessa at Cambridge. They were both students there. At first she didn't like him very much, but later they became good friends.

After Tessa got her degree, she went to Spain for a year, where she taught English. After that she found a job with an advertising agency in London called Bell and Winter. She worked there for two years and then got a job with Knight and Day. She is now twenty-nine years old.

After Roger left university, he found a job with a computer company in Boston. He didn't work there very long. A year later he left and got a job with another company in San Francisco. Roger is now thirty years old.

1

Complete these questions about Tessa and Roger. Then answer them.

1 Where was ＿＿ born?
2 Was ＿＿ born in ＿＿, too?
3 Where did ＿＿ grow up?
4 What about ＿＿?
5 When did ＿＿ come back to ＿＿?
6 What did ＿＿ do when she/he was ＿＿?

• Now think of more questions, and answer them, too.

2

Say something about Roger or Tessa that you know is wrong. Can another student correct it?

Example: A: Tessa was born in London.
B: No, she wasn't born in London. She was born in Liverpool.

Developing language

Grammar: Past Simple

1

Look at the sentences below about Roger. What is different about you?

Example: Roger was born in London.
– I wasn't born in London. I was born in . . .

1 He grew up in San Francisco.
2 He went to school there, too.
3 He had a dog when he was a boy. It was called Sam.
4 He started school when he was five.
5 He liked school very much.
6 He thought it was wonderful.
7 He liked all his teachers, too.
8 When he was younger he wanted to be a chemist.
9 He enjoyed sports, too, and played baseball and basketball.

2 *Writing*

Write all the things that Roger did but that you didn't do.

I wasn't born in London. I didn't...

3 *Groupwork*

Get as much information as you can about other people in your class. Ask questions like these.

Where were you born?

Did you grow up there, too?

Where did you go to school?

Did you like school very much?

4

Now tell one student about another student in the class.

Example: – . . . was born in . . .
– He/She grew up in . . .
– She/He went to school in . . .

☞ See Grammar Summary 16, pages 83–84.

Vocabulary: *get*

5

Look at these examples. What is the meaning of *get* in each sentence?

1 Did you get that information I wanted?
2 When do we get to Munich?
3 It's getting very cold.
4 Why are you laughing? I don't get it.
5 Roger got a job in Boston after he left Cambridge.

6

You can't use *get* or *gets* in two of these sentences. Can you find them?

1 When do you usually ____ home in the evening?
2 It usually ____ very warm here in the summer.
3 Where can I ____ some food?
4 Don't ____ angry.
5 I wanted to talk to Tessa, but I couldn't ____ her on the phone.
6 I'm studying medicine. I want to ____ a doctor.
7 I feel terrible. I don't know what's wrong with me. Please ____ a doctor.
8 Can you ____ a taxi for me, please?
9 I'd like to discuss that with you. Let's ____ lunch together tomorrow.

Pronunciation: /g/ get or /dʒ/ jet 📼

7

a) **Say these words. How do you say the letter in bold?**

jet **j**ob **J**ack **j**eans

b) **Now say these words. Which ones have the same sound in them as 'j' in the four words above?**

1 agency manager get Cambridge
2 large larger bigger Roger
3 age suggest intelligent subjects
4 gentleman general July jazz
5 Japan Germany Egypt Belgium

c) **Listen and check.**

Flying to San Francisco

Conversation

Two people are talking. They are on a plane from Tokyo to San Francisco.

ROGER: Are you from San Francisco?
ANNE: No, but I lived there for five years before I went to Japan.
ROGER: Oh. How long were you there? In Japan, I mean.
ANNE: Oh, for about three years.
ROGER: And did you like it?
ANNE: Yes, I did. Very much.
ROGER: What did you do there?
ANNE: I designed European-style restaurants. I worked for a company in Tokyo that specialises in that.
ROGER: Oh, did you? Hmm.
ANNE: But what about you? What do you do?
ROGER: I'm an engineer. I work for a company that makes software.
ANNE: Oh, do you? What kind of software?
ROGER: The type architects use when they design buildings.
ANNE: Oh, really? Perhaps it's like the software I used in Japan.
ROGER: Yes, it probably is. Uh . . . what do you plan to do now?
ANNE: Well, if possible, I'd like to find a job in San Francisco. Something like the job I had in Tokyo, I mean.
ROGER: Sometimes I hear about things like that. Perhaps . . . uh . . . I can help you. Here's my card.
ANNE: Oh, that's very kind of you. Thanks.

1

Find words or phrases in the conversation that mean these things.

1 to do or to study only one thing
2 not exactly the same, but very close
3 something with a person's name, name of his or her company, address and telephone number on it

2

Now find these sentences in the conversation. What's the full meaning of the word in *italics*?

1 Yes, I *did*. Very much.
2 Oh, *do* you? What kind of software?
3 Yes, it probably *is*.

3

Say one or two sentences about these things.

Example: • Anne before she went to Tokyo
– She lived in San Francisco for five years.

  • Anne's job in Tokyo
  • her plans
  • Roger and his job
  • how he can help Anne

Listening

4

Listen. Then answer these questions.

1 Who is speaking?
2 Who is he speaking to?
3 Where are they going?
4 How long does it take to get there?
5 What time is it now?
6 When do they arrive?

Exploring language

Grammar: short answers

1

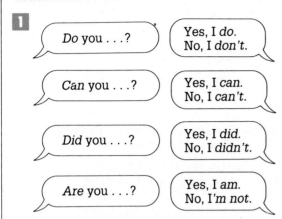

Do you . . .?   Yes, I do.
                 No, I don't.

Can you . . .?   Yes, I can.
                 No, I can't.

Did you . . .?   Yes, I did.
                 No, I didn't.

Are you . . .?   Yes, I am.
                 No, I'm not.

Study the examples above. Then answer the questions about yourself.

Example: Do you live in England?
– Yes, I do./ No, I don't.

1 Are you listening?
2 Do you live very far from here?
3 Did you know any English before you began this course?
4 Can you drive?
5 Are you married?
6 Do you like jazz?

• Here are some more questions. Answer them in the same way.

1 Were you here yesterday?
2 Have you got a car?
3 Was it very cold yesterday?
4 Is this kind of exercise very difficult for you?

Grammar: short questions to show interest

2

Look at what B says. How does it show that B is interested in what A is saying?

A (I lived in China   Did you? In which) B
    for two years.   part of China?

• A also says these things. What do you think B says?

1 I can speak three foreign languages.
2 My sister is married to a film star.
3 I had a very bad day yesterday.
4 I hate my job.
5 I don't like learning English.

Vocabulary: words with two meanings

3

Look at the examples. Is the meaning of the word in *italics* the same or different?

1 I *like* pizza.
  It's *like* pizza.
2 That's very *kind* of you.
  What *kind* of food do you like?
3 My company *makes* software.
  A good engineer can *make* a lot of money these days.

• Look at the second example of each question again. Find another way of saying the same thing.

Example: It's *like* pizza.
           – It's almost the same as pizza.

4

Complete these sentences with words from exercise 3.

1 In some ways English is ＿＿ German, but in other ways the two languages are very different.
2 Ford and Honda both ＿＿ cars.
3 A: What ＿＿ of work do you do?
   B: I'm an architect.
4 It's very ＿＿ of you to help me.
5 Last year was very bad for our company. We didn't ＿＿ any money at all.

Pronunciation: /s/ this or /z/ is 🔊

5

a) Which words have the sound /z/?

1 design sign music easy
2 is this these those
3 does was his it's
4 hats books clients jobs
5 things thinks friends arguments

b) Now listen and check.

c) Only one word in each phrase has a /z/ sound. Which one?

• Architects use this software.
• It's easy to say seven.
• Sue likes this music.
• This shop sold a thousand tickets last Saturday.

I'd like your opinion

1 Which sentence is an opinion?

• London is more beautiful than Paris.

• London is in England.

2 Which of these things do people say when they give an opinion?
   a) I think . . .
   b) I know . . .
   c) I believe . . .

Conversation

Tessa Saunders is talking to David Kale, the Publicity Director of Artaud International, a French sportswear company.

TESSA: Thank you for lunch, David.
DAVID: Did you enjoy it?
TESSA: Yes, I did. Very much.
DAVID: I'm glad we could meet today. I'd like to talk to you about . . . about . . . um . . . I hope you understand this is all very confidential?
TESSA: Of course.
DAVID: It's about the agency that does our advertising for us.
TESSA: Bell and Winter?
DAVID: Yes. You worked for them once, didn't you?
TESSA: Yes, I did. Four years ago.
DAVID: Hmm. What did you think of them?
TESSA: What did I think of them?
DAVID: Yes. I'd like your opinion.
TESSA: I don't really think my opinion is very useful any more.
DAVID: Why not?
TESSA: Because, as I said, I left the agency four years ago. A lot can change in that time.
DAVID: Yes, but . . .
TESSA: Now, come on, David. You're their client. Why don't you tell me what you think of them?

1

Do you agree with these explanations?

1 People can *enjoy* food but not music.
2 *It's confidential* means 'don't tell other people about this'.
3 *This isn't useful* means 'this can really help you'.

2

Can you find the question it is not possible to answer? Answer the others.

1 Who or what are Bell and Winter?
2 How long ago did Tessa work there?
3 David asks her two questions about them. Which one do you think is more important?
4 What is Tessa's opinion of Bell and Winter?

Listening

3

Listen to the complete conversation. Then answer these questions.

1 Why is David talking to Tessa about Bell and Winter?
2 What does she want to do when she goes back to her office?

Developing language

Grammar: *for/ago*

1

Study these facts.

- Tessa is now 29 years old.
- She got a job with Bell and Winter when she was 23.
- She left Bell and Winter when she was 25.

- Now say which sentence below is true.

She worked for Bell and Winter four years ago.

She worked for Bell and Winter for four years.

2

Read the things Tessa did. Then say how long ago she did them. (She is 29 now.)

Example: She started university when she was 18.
— She started university eleven years ago.

1 She met Roger when she was 18.
2 She left university when she was 21.
3 She went to Spain when she was 22.
4 She left Spain when she was 23.
5 She got a job with Knight and Day when she was 25.

- How long did she study at university?
- How long do people usually study at university in your country?

3 *What about you?*

Use these sentences to say something about yourself.

1 I began learning English ____ ago.
2 I got my first job ____ ago.
3 I started school ____ ago.
4 I left school ____ ago.
5 I began using this book ____ ago.

- Think about other important things you did at different times in your life. How long ago did you do them?

4

Say something you did four years ago which is true and something which is false. Don't say which one is true or false. Let other people guess.

Example: Four years ago I was the director of a big international bank.
— False./– True.

☞ See Grammar Summary 17, page 84.

Vocabulary: feelings

5

How many of these words do you know? Can you use them in sentences?

glad or *happy*
1 I'm ____ to see you.
2 I'm very ____ in my new job.

sad or *sorry*
3 I'm ____ to hear that you lost your job.
4 Why are you so ____ today? What's wrong?

sad or *unlucky*
5 Some people think that the number thirteen is ____ .
6 What a ____ story!

happy or *lucky*
7 Everybody at the party was very ____ .
8 You're never ill. You have no problems. You're a very ____ person!

Pronunciation: /juː/ you

6

a) One part of these words has the sound /juː/. Which part is it?

1 useful   5 few
2 usually   6 beautiful
3 music   7 interview
4 excuse   8 argue

b) Now listen and check.

More problems

1 How many of the phrases on the right do you know?
2 Which phrases here do we often use at the beginning of a conversation?
3 Which phrases here do we often use at the end of a conversation?
4 What about the other phrases here? When can you use them?

> Please.
>
> Nice day today, isn't it?
>
> How are things?
>
> Take care.
>
> How's life?
>
> See you later.
>
> Good morning. How are you today?
>
> Bye.
>
> Warmer today, isn't it?
>
> Could you . . .?
>
> Thanks.
>
> Is it possible to . . .?
>
> Would you . . .?
>
> Have a good day.

Reading

These letters are from a popular British magazine.

> My boss has no idea of what the word 'polite' really means. He says, 'Do this!' or 'Do that!', but never says, 'Please' or 'Thank you'.
> When I make a small mistake, he says, 'This is very bad!' or 'I don't like this!', but he never explains what is wrong or why he doesn't like it.
> He never smiles and he doesn't even say, 'Hello' or 'How are you today?' in the morning.
> What should I do? Should I tell him why I am so unhappy? Or should I look for another job?
> *Nora, Southampton*

> I'd like to get a job in Germany very soon, but I don't speak German. One of my friends says this isn't really necessary because most Germans speak good English.
> What do you think? Should I learn German? Isn't it better to speak the language if I want to work there? And how should I do it? I mean, how can I learn German in only a few months? What's the best way?
> *Chris, Bristol*

1

Answer the questions.

1 Why does Nora say her boss has *no idea of what the word 'polite' really means*?
2 What are the things he does that she doesn't like?
3 Why does Chris want to learn German?
4 What does Chris want to know?

2 *Groupwork*

Give your opinion about these things. Find out what other people in your class think, too.

1 Do you think Nora's boss is a good or a bad manager? Or do you think it isn't possible to say? Give reasons.
2 What do you think is the best way to learn a foreign language?
3 You are someone's boss. They make a small mistake. How do you tell them about it?

Exploring language

Grammar: *should*

1

Look at the picture and answer these questions.

1 What is one person doing that is wrong?
2 What are the most important words that the other person is saying?

No Smoking

> Excuse me, but you shouldn't smoke here.

2

Say what they should do.

Example: Chris wants to live in Germany, but he doesn't speak German.
– He should learn German.

1 I want to live in France, but I don't speak French.
2 Mário wants to read English books, but he hasn't got a good dictionary.
3 Tessa always feels tired in the morning, but she always goes to bed very late.
4 Roger wants to see Anne again. She gave him her telephone number.
5 Nora's boss never says, 'Thank you' or 'Please' and he never explains what is wrong with her work.

3

Say what you really think. Use *should* or *shouldn't*.

1 Women ____ get the same pay as men if they do the same job.
2 A man ____ earn more money than a woman for the same job.
3 You ____ drink alcohol when you drive.
4 If you see the words 'No Smoking' in a room, it means that you ____ smoke there.
5 Nora ____ tell her boss why she is unhappy.

 See Grammar Summary 20, page 85.

Vocabulary: *say and tell*

4

Study the examples. Then answer the questions about them.

1 One of my friends *says* that most Germans speak English.

2 One of my friends *tells* me that most Germans speak English.

3 'That's not right,' another friend *says*.

4 Another friend *tells* me that isn't right.

• Should you use *say* or *tell* when the word that comes next is a word like *me*?
• Which of these words are the same kind of word as *me*?
  us   her   she   he   him   they   them

5

***say* or *tell*?**

1 Do you always ____ 'Good morning'?
2 Excuse me. Can you ____ me the way to Oxford Street?
3 Pardon? What did you ____?
4 What's wrong? ____ me!
5 Why doesn't Nora's boss ____ her what is wrong?

Pronunciation

6

a) When is the sound different?

1 old   cold   should   hold
2 should   good   food   would
3 thousand   how   about   four
4 now   thousand   mouth   fourth
5 or   work   sport   four
6 work   were   here   her

b) Now listen and check.

Conversation 📼

Someone on the phone wants to talk to Tessa.

CALLER: Hello. This is Paula Silverman. I'd like to speak to Tessa Saunders, please.

PENNY: I'm afraid she's away on a business trip. Would you like to leave a message, um . . . Sorry, what was your name again?

CALLER: Paula Silverman. I'm with Metro Radio. I'd like to interview her on my programme.

PENNY: Oh, I see. What would you like to interview her about?

CALLER: I'd like to explain that to her myself. Could she phone me? Could you ask her to do that?

PENNY: Yes, of course. Could I have your number, please?

CALLER: Yes, it's oh seven one, two . . . no, just a moment. It's probably better if I phone her. When will she be back?

PENNY: On Monday.

CALLER: All right. I'll phone her sometime on Monday morning.

Before you begin

1 What do you usually do when your phone rings?
a) answer it   b) hang up
c) take it   d) something else
2 What do people usually do when they take a message?
a) lie down   b) hold it
c) write something down

1

Find the words or phrases in the conversation that mean these things.

1 something you can hear on the radio
2 a phrase that really means 'You told me your name, but I can't remember it, or perhaps I didn't hear it.'
3 a word that means 'I don't know exactly when'

2

Answer these questions.

1 Who wants to talk to Tessa?
2 Why does she want to talk to her?
3 What will Penny's message be?
4 When will she give it to Tessa?

Listening 📼

3

Listen to a conversation between Penny and another caller. Then look at the message below. Can you find any mistakes in it?

To:	Tessa
From:	Penny
Re:	Metro Radio Interview
Date:	4 March

A Miss Grazziela Banci (?) from Milan phoned. You met her there last month. She is an artist and would like to show you some of her new work. She will be in London from 13th March to 6th April and would like to arrange a meeting with you. You can phone her in Milan on 27163449 or here in London after 30th on 081 457 6997.

Developing language

Grammar: *could*

1

Look at these examples of *could*. Is the meaning always the same?

1 Mozart could play the piano when he was only four years old.

2 Could you repeat that? I didn't understand.

3 Could you phone me later?

4 Could you speak English very well when you were ten years old?

2

Which sentence do you think is more polite in this situation?

- Answer that phone.
- Could you answer that phone, please?

3

Say these things in a more polite way with *could*.

Example: Come to my office for a minute.
– Could you come to my office for a minute, please?

1 Take this to the director's office.
2 Get this information for me.
3 Turn that radio down.
4 Wait a minute.
5 Explain this to me.

☞ See Grammar Summary 21, page 85.

Vocabulary: travel

4

Match the words with the definitions.

- flight
- journey
- travel
- voyage
- trip

1 ____ *verb*: to go from one place to another place
2 ____ *noun*: a word we use when we are talking about travelling a long distance, usually by land
3 ____ *noun*: a journey or trip by air
4 ____ *noun*: a journey or trip by sea
5 ____ *noun*: a word we often use when we travel for business, pleasure or for shopping

5

Use the same five words about travel to complete these sentences.

1 Tessa is away on a business ____.
2 Do you ____ very much in your job?
3 British Airways wish you a pleasant ____.
4 The ____ by train from Liverpool to London takes about three hours.
5 When I was very young, my parents took me on a long ____ across the Pacific Ocean.

Vocabulary: take or go on

6

Which of these things can you *take*? Which can you *go on*?

- a shower
- a trip
- a bus
- a taxi
- a bath
- a seat
- your time
- a message
- lessons in business English
- a test
- a voyage
- a plane

Pronunciation

7

a) All these words and phrases have the same sound. Which sound is it?

1 yest**er**day
2 inf**or**mation
3 photograph**er**
4 **a**go
5 **a**bout
6 **a**gain
7 you **and** I
8 tea **and** coffee
9 phone h**er** t**o**day

b) Now listen and check.

Messages

Reading

These messages will be on Tessa's desk when she gets back on Monday.

> **To:** Tessa
>
> **From:** Penny
>
> **Re:** Interview on Metro Radio
>
> **Date:** 4 March
>
> Paula Silverman of Metro Radio phoned this morning. She wants to interview you on her programme.
> She will phone you on Monday morning to find out if you are interested.

> **To:** Tessa
>
> **From:** Richard
>
> **Re:** Your conversation with David Kale
>
> **Date:** 4 March
>
> **Confidential**
>
> Thanks for the information about Artaud International. We should make a decision about this as soon as possible. Let's meet on Monday morning to discuss this.

> FAX transmission to Tessa Saunders, Knight and Day, London 010-44-71-342-6977
>
> from Thanos Constantinides, Athens
>
> Number of pages in this transmission: 1
>
> 4 March
>
> Urgent.
> I have several questions regarding the documents you want me to translate into Greek for you. Could you phone me on Monday morning at 10 am, your time, or if this is not convenient for you, between 8 am and 3 pm your time on Tuesday?

1

Do you agree with these explanations?

1 Someone who says 'I will do this and not that' is *making a decision*.
2 *As soon as possible* means 'You have a lot of time to do this.'
3 A letter *regarding* (*Re.*) a decision is a letter about that decision.
4 When people say *This is urgent*, they mean 'Take your time. I can wait.'
5 When you *translate* a letter, you read it in one language and write it in another language.

2

Answer the questions.

1 What are three things Tessa will probably do on Monday morning?
2 What is at least one question Paula Silverman will ask her?
3 What will she talk about with Richard?
4 What will she talk about with Thanos Constantinides?

Listening

3

Listen to the conversation. Then answer these questions.

1 Who are the two speakers?
2 What is the message one of the speakers leaves?

Writing

4

Read the note that Tessa gives Penny on Monday.

- What do you think Penny writes to Graziella? Write the complete fax.

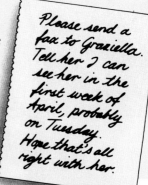

Please send a fax to Graziella. Tell her I can see her in the first week of April, probably on Tuesday. Hope that's all right with her.

Exploring language

Grammar: *will*

1

Look at the three pairs of examples. How does the meaning change?

1 The messages *are* on your desk.
The messages *will be* on your desk.

2 *Is* the traffic very heavy?
Will the traffic *be* very heavy?

3 People *don't* understand this.
People *won't* understand this.

- Find a sentence above that could mean these things.

Can you see a lot of cars on the road now?

What about the traffic tomorrow?

- What about the other sentences? How are they different? What do they mean?

2

Change from *today* to *tomorrow*.

Example: The traffic is very heavy today.
– The traffic will be very heavy tomorrow.

1 The food is good today.
2 Is the food good today?
3 You like it today.
4 Do you like it today?
5 You don't like it today.

3

Change *now* to *later* in these sentences. What other change is necessary?

1 You understand this now.
2 I don't need this now.
3 Are you satisfied now?

4 *Writing*

Write down three or four sentences about things you *usually* do on Sunday. Begin this way.

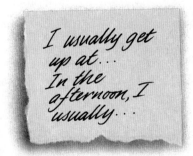

*I usually get up at...
In the afternoon, I usually...*

Now write three or four sentences about next Sunday. Begin this way.

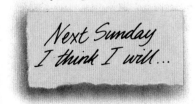

Next Sunday I think I will...

See Grammar Summary 22, page 86.

Vocabulary: *-ing* and *-ed* adjectives

5

Discuss the difference.

This is very interesting.

Are you interested in this?

- Which explanation is completely wrong?

1 We use *interesting* only when we are talking about things. People are always *interested*, never *interesting*.
2 If you are *interested*, it means you want to know more about something or someone.
3 If you are *interesting*, it usually means that people want to know more about you.

6

Complete the sentences.

interested or *interesting*
1 That woman over there looks very ____. I'd really like to meet her.
2 We were all very ____ in your talk.

bored or *boring*
3 I was so ____ that I went to sleep in the middle of the film.
4 It was a very ____ film.

satisifed or *satisfying*
5 My job is very ____.
6 I'm very ____ with my job.

11 It doesn't work

Before you begin

1 Explain the difference in the meaning of *work* in these sentences.
   • Mary doesn't *work* here any more.
   • This camera doesn't *work*.
2 Yesterday you bought an expensive camera from a good shop. Today it doesn't work. Explain what you will do next.

Conversation

Tessa Saunders is in Munich today. She is meeting Manfred Kernholz, the Marketing Director of T.R.S., and Frau Fischer, the Publicity Director.

TESSA: What are the most important things we can say about the new video camera?

KERNHOLZ: Frau Fischer. Would you like to answer that question?

FISCHER: First of all, it will be one of the best cameras on the market. But it won't be the most expensive.

TESSA: Just a moment, please. I'd like to make some notes. Where's my pen? Here it is. Yes, go on, please.

FISCHER: You see, we are using some completely new materials. This means that the camera will also be one of the lightest and smallest on the market. But the quality of the pictures and also the sound is excellent.

TESSA: Oh, no!

KERNHOLZ: What's the matter?

TESSA: My pen! I bought it only two days ago. It cost a lot, but it doesn't work!

KERNHOLZ: Can I lend you my pen?

TESSA: No, that's all right. I've got another one with me. Thanks all the same.

1

Answer the questions.

1 Why does Frau Fischer talk about the video camera in the future and not in the present tense?
2 What exactly do you think Tessa began doing after she said *I'd like to make some notes*?
3 Talk about some situations when people say *Just a moment, please*.
4 Why does Herr Kernholz ask *What's the matter?*
5 Talk about some other situations when people ask *What's the matter?*

Writing

2

What notes do you think Tessa made? Write them.

Listening

3

Listen to the conversation that Tessa and Kernholz have before the meeting. Then answer these questions.

1 What are the questions that Kernholz asks Tessa?
2 Do you think these questions are important in a situation like this? Give reasons.

Developing language

Grammar: superlatives

1

Compare the cars.

A £10,000

B £300

C £45,000

1 Which car is the most expensive?
2 Which one is the cheapest?
3 Match the cars with these descriptions.
   • the fastest   • the slowest
   • the most comfortable
   • the least comfortable

2

These three people all want to buy a car. Study the information about them.

Alex, 20, student with 3 girlfriends. Very rich.

Mary, 37. One child and an old mother who lives with her. Drives short distances in a big city.

Ruth, 52, company director. Married with 2 children. Often drives long distances to see very important clients.

• Now discuss these questions.

1 Which car in exercise 1 do you think is the best for each person? Why?
2 Which car do you think is the worst for each person? Why?
3 Which car would be best for you? Why?

> ☞ See Grammar Summary 19, page 85.

Vocabulary: *lend* or *borrow*

3

Look at the picture and answer the questions.

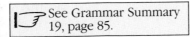

A   B

1 Who is lending money? A or B?
2 Who is borrowing it?
3 What is A doing? What is B doing?

4

Study the definitions and examples.

> **lend** v **lent** to give someone something for a limited time: *Can you lend me £10? I'll return it next week. I lent her my dictionary; she'll bring it back tomorrow.*

> **borrow** to take or receive something for a certain time, intending to return it: *Can I borrow £10 from you? I'll give it back to you tomorrow.*

5

lend or *borrow*?

1 I haven't got enough money to buy the car. Perhaps I can ____ some more from the bank.
2 How much money do you need? Maybe I can ____ it to you.
3 Could you ____ me your dictionary for a minute?
4 Could I ____ that pen, too?

Pronunciation: *I'll do* or *I do* 📼

6

a) Say these phrases.

A   B

I do it.   I'll do it.
They like it.   They'll like it.
We discuss it.   We'll discuss it.

b) Now listen. Do you hear a sentence like A or a sentence like B?

Example: I'll do it.
– B.

High-tech

Before you begin

1 How many different electronic products can you name?
2 Where are these products usually made?
3 Name some electronic products you have or would like to have.

Reading

This article appeared in an English newspaper a few days after Tessa came back from Munich.

New 'Spy' Camera

A new video camera from T.R.S. will soon be in the shops. It is made of strong but very light high-tech materials and it is so small that you can easily carry it with you wherever you go.

There will be two models of the camera, the Compact and the Super. The Compact is even smaller and lighter than the Super.

One of the most unusual features of the Super is its high quality sound recording system. 'Let's say you are at a party. You are at one side of a large room and two people are talking at the other side. You can focus not only the picture, but also the sound, and hear them very clearly. The recording quality is also unusually high,' Barbara Fischer, the Publicity Director, said.

1

Do you agree with these explanations?

1 *Soon* means 'a long time in the future'.
2 The phrase *in the shops* in this text means more or less the same as 'on the market'.
3 Cotton, steel and plastic are *materials*.
4 Things that you can *easily carry* are usually very heavy.
5 The meaning of the word *features* changes if you say, 'This machine has some nice features' and 'I like your face. You have very nice features.'
6 It is unusual to find something of very *high quality* and a very low price.

2

Answer the questions.

1 What features of the new camera do you think people will like?
2 Let's say that you work for Company A and you are at a party. You can see the Director of Company B at the same party. The two companies make similar products. You have the T.R.S. Super with you. What do you do?

3 *What about you?*

Describe something you have. It can be a machine, some clothing or even the place where you live. What are the features you like about it? Are there any features you don't like?

4 *Roleplay*

A: You are a salesperson in a shop that sells video cameras. B is a customer and is looking at the T.R.S. Compact. Find out why B wants a video camera. Then decide which model is better for her/him: the Super or the Compact.

B: You are the customer. You want a camera you can use to take videos of your friends and family. But you would also like to hear what people who work in the same office with you say about you. Ask A about it.

Exploring language

Grammar: adjectives and adverbs

1

Study the examples and answer the questions about them.

Adjective	Adverb
1 Your English is very *good*.	You speak English very *well*.
2 I'm a *bad* dancer.	I dance *badly*.
3 Your writing isn't very *clear*.	Please write *clearly*.
4 It isn't *possible*.	I can't *possibly* do it.
5 You're a very *fast* worker.	You work very *fast*.

- What are some examples of adjectives?
- What are some examples of adverbs?
- Which do we use with a noun – an adjective or an adverb?
- Which form do we use with a verb?
- There is a word here that has the same adjective and adverb form. What is it?

2

Choose the correct form.

clear or *clearly*
1 This explanation isn't very ___.
2 How can we explain this more ___.

good or *well*
3 She works ___ with other people.
4 She is a ___ colleague.

bad or *badly*
5 At first the meeting went ___.
6 The weather is very ___ today.

possible or *possibly*
7 How can this be ___?
8 I will come at 7, or ___ at 7.15.

What's the missing word here?

9 You're driving too ___. Slow down!
10 I bought a new Porsche last week. It's very ___.

 See Grammar Summary 25, page 87.

Vocabulary: materials

3

Find the word that doesn't belong.

1 steel   wood   hard   plastic
2 cotton   wool   nylon   soft
3 clothes   silk   leather   suede
4 chair   table   carpet   smooth
5 cloth   gold   silver   platinum

4

Look at the people around you. Who is wearing these materials?

wool   cotton   nylon   silk   gold   leather

- What things are made of these materials?
- What other materials can you see around you?
- What are the names of the things that are made of these other materials?

5

Read these two descriptions of different materials. Perhaps you don't understand every word, but can you say what the material is?

> This material isn't very hard, but it isn't very soft either. It can be white or brown or other colours. The pages of a book are made of it.

> **This material is hard, but not always very hard. It is usually smooth, too. It is used to make all kinds of things in different shapes – round things and square things. Cups and plates are sometimes made of this material, but they are usually cheap.**

Writing

6

Write a description of another material in the same way. Can your partner tell you the name of the material you describe?

Tomorrow isn't good enough!

Conversation

Roger Mitchum works for a computer software company in San Francisco. He is talking to his boss, Dell Bradford. They are talking about Mr Yamada, their distributor in Japan.

ROGER: Yamada thinks he can increase sales of the new software, but he . . .

BRADFORD: How much?

ROGER: Pardon?

BRADFORD: How much of an increase is he talking about? Did he tell you?

ROGER: It's in my report.

BRADFORD: Yeah, but where's the report? I have to see it, Roger.

ROGER: I'm sorry. I'll finish it as soon as possible.

BRADFORD: Tell me. How do you feel today, Roger?

ROGER: I . . . I'm all right. Why?

BRADFORD: Are you tired?

ROGER: No, not at all . . .

BRADFORD: Tense? Nervous? Worried, perhaps?

ROGER: No.

BRADFORD: Well, you should be, Roger. Because I'm not happy at all. I'm tense and I'm worried. Do you know why?

ROGER: I suppose it's because . . .

BRADFORD: No, don't tell me. I'll tell you why, Roger. I have to know things. Important things. And you aren't telling me them.

ROGER: But they're all in my report. I'll finish it as soon as possible.

BRADFORD: That isn't good enough, Roger. I want it now. Do you understand? Not 'as soon possible'.

1

Answer the questions.

1 What kind of information is in the report?
2 How does Bradford feel?
3 Why does he feel this way?
4 What does he want Roger to do?

2

Can you answer these, too?

1 What will Roger do after he leaves the office?
2 How do you think he feels?
3 Is Bradford's way of speaking to people a good way for managers or directors to talk to people? Give reasons.

Listening

3

Listen to the complete conversation. Then answer the questions.

1 What does Roger do at the end of his conversation with Bradford?
2 Who do you think Mary is?
3 What is the confidential information Bradford gives her?

Developing language

Grammar: *have to*

1

All these examples are about the future. But there is an important difference between them. What is it?

1 (We *can* increase our sales in Japan.)

2 (We *will* increase our sales in Japan.)

3 (We *have to* increase our sales in Japan.)

- Find sentences above that mean these things.

a) It is possible to do this.
b) It is necessary to do this.
c) You can be sure about this.

2

Study these examples. How many sentences can you make?

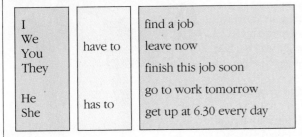

I We You They He She	have to has to	find a job leave now finish this job soon go to work tomorrow get up at 6.30 every day

3

Change the meaning from 'I'm sure' to 'It's necessary'.

Example: I'll do this tomorrow.
        – I have to do this tomorrow.

1 I'll see a doctor tomorrow.
2 I'll give the boss my report tomorrow.
3 Roger will finish his report this evening.
4 Tessa will be in Seville tomorrow.
5 We'll finish all this work before we leave.
6 Roger's report will be on Bradford's desk tomorrow morning.
7 You will finish this book soon.
8 Now we will do a little more practice.

4 *What about you?*

Read these questions and answer them.

1 Do you have to learn English for your job?

2 Do you have to use a typewriter or a word-processor every day?

3 Do you have to get up early every morning?

4 Do you have to travel very far to get to work or school?

☞ See Grammar Summary 24, pages 86–87.

Vocabulary: feelings

5

How many of these words do you know?

tired   angry   relaxed   nervous   tense
worried   happy   in a good mood   depressed

- Talk about how you feel in these situations.

  - just before an examination or an interview
  - when you have money problems
  - when it rains and rains and never stops
  - when the sun comes out after the rain
  - at the moment

Pronunciation: weak forms

6

a) **In which examples should you use the weak forms of *have* ('ve) or *has* ('s)? Can you find two examples in which you should not use the weak forms?**

1 We have got a problem here.
2 Mary's here. She has got a question for you.
3 Bill's here, too. He has got a question, too.
4 They have got a lot of questions.
5 I'm afraid you have to see them now.
6 Mary has to leave in a minute.

b) **Now listen and check.**

Ambition

1 Which of these phrases can you use when you talk about your
    ambitions?
a) I often worry about . . .
b) I'm very sorry that I didn't . . .
c) Someday I hope that I will . . .

2 Talk about your ambitions when you were younger. How are they
    different from your ambitions now?

Reading

This is part of a magazine article about Dell Bradford, the director of
a software company in San Francisco.

**One day, when Dell Bradford was sixteen years old and still at high school,
a teacher asked everyone in his class the same question: 'What do you want
to be when you're older?'**

The other students all gave answers like 'engineer', 'doctor', 'lawyer' or
'teacher'. But Bradford said, 'A millionaire.'

'That wasn't my real ambition. I didn't want to tell anyone about that,'
he says.

A few years later, Bradford went to university, where he got a degree
in computer engineering. Then, at the age of twenty-three, he borrowed
some money from a friend and started his own software company.
When he was twenty-seven he was a millionaire. But what was his real
ambition when he was sixteen, and why didn't he want to tell anyone
about it?

'I was always the shortest kid at school and I wanted to be at least six
inches (15 centimetres) taller. But after the teacher asked me that
question, I realized something. I couldn't do anything about my height.
But I could do something about other things in my life. I could even
become a millionaire if I tried hard enough,' he answers.

1

Discuss the words and meanings.

1 How old are most of the people in a *high school*?
2 Where do people go in America to get a *degree* in
    something? A department store? A drug store? Or
    somewhere else?
3 Where do people go in your country if they want
    to *borrow* money?
4 What is the word in the text that means 'believe
    or understand something you didn't believe or
    understand before'?

2

What can you say about these things?

● Dell Bradford's real ambition when he was
   sixteen
● the ambitions of the other people in his class
● two of the important things that happened in his
   life later
● the important thing he realised after the teacher
   asked him about his ambition

3 *Groupwork*

**Find out how many people in your class
would like to have a million dollars. Then
find out what they would like to do with the
money.**

Exploring language

Grammar: *something/anything/ nothing*

Study these examples. Then answer the questions.

1 *Something* is wrong with this machine.
2 I'm sorry, but I can't find *anything* wrong with this machine.
3 There's *nothing* wrong with it. *Nothing*!

- Which word do we use when the sentence is already negative?
- Which word do we use when we want to say 'a thing' and not give the name of the thing?
- Which word means something like 'zero'?

something, *anything* or *nothing*?

1 I'm very hungry, but there's ____ to eat.
2 I don't want to eat ____.
3 Here's ____ for you, Mary, and ____ for you, Peter.
4 I think you want to tell me ____. What is it?
5 No, I really don't want to say ____.
6 ____ in life is more important than your health. ____! It's the most important thing there is.
7 A: Pardon? What did you say?
   B: ____.
8 I can see ____ under the table. What is it?
9 Really? I can't see ____ there at all.

> ☞ See Grammar Summary 26, page 87.

Pronunciation: stress and weak forms 📼

Say these words, first alone and then in phrases and sentences. How does the pronunciation change?

1 some/ some letters/ There are some letters here.
2 for/ for me/ Is this letter for me?
3 from/ from his father/ He borrowed some money from his father.
4 than/ more important than your health/ There is nothing more important than your health.
5 them/ see them now/ Can you see them now?
6 him/ see him now/ Can you see him now?

b) Now listen and check.

Vocabulary: dimensions

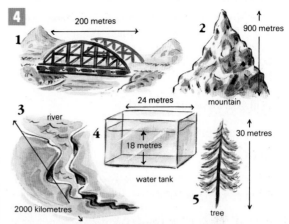

Do you know the words for the pictures above? Are they *tall*, *high*, *wide*, *long* or *deep*?

Now complete the sentences. Use these words.

- tall   - deep   - high   - heavy   - short   - long

1 How ____ is that mountain?
2 That child is as ____ as a man!
3 The water is very ____. I can't see the bottom.
4 This suitcase is very ____. I can't carry it.
5 Your hair is very ____. Why don't you get a haircut?
6 She looks like a man because her hair is so ____.

Writing

What do you hope will happen in the next five years? Write at least three sentences.

Example:

I hope I will have a better
job than I have now.
I also hope there won't be
any more wars.
I hope the world will be a
safer place than it is today.

13 Profit and loss

1 You buy something for a thousand dollars and sell it for two thousand dollars. What do you call the difference in the two prices?
2 Look at these two questions. Do you think there is a difference in meaning?

> Will you have dinner with me?

> Are you going to have dinner with me?

Conversation 📼

Tessa Saunders and Richard Knight are talking about a company called Artaud International. At the moment, the company is the client of another advertising agency.

RICHARD: Yes, that's very interesting, Tessa. Now what do you know about their financial situation?
TESSA: Well, they didn't do too well last year. They lost a lot of money in the first half. But the second half was better.
RICHARD: I'd like exact figures.
TESSA: I'll get them if I can.
RICHARD: Are they going to make a profit this year?
TESSA: It's difficult to . . .
RICHARD: I know what you're going to say. It's difficult to know because the year isn't over yet. Just get as much information as possible.
TESSA: I'll do my best.
RICHARD: Are they going to bring out any new products this year? Find out about that, too.
TESSA: All right. Anything else?
RICHARD: No, not for the moment. Oh . . . uh . . . by the way, what are your plans for tomorrow evening?
TESSA: Well, I'm going to do an interview at Metro Radio early in the evening. Why?
RICHARD: My partner from New York is going to be here. There's something very important we'd like to discuss with you.
TESSA: Oh! In the evening?
RICHARD: Yes. Will you have dinner with us?

1

Discuss the meanings of these words.

1 What is the opposite of *profit*?
2 Which word is very different here?
   • numbers • figures • products • statistics
3 Explain the difference in the meaning of *partner* in these sentences.
   • Tessa came to the party with her new *partner*.
   • John Bell and Michael Winter are *partners*. They started their agency in 1972.

2

Answer these questions, too.

1 Explain what Tessa means when she says that Artaud International *didn't do too well last year*.
2 What else does Richard want to know?
3 What are Tessa's plans for tomorrow evening?
4 Why does Richard want to see her in the evening?

Listening 📼

3

Listen to the complete conversation. Then answer the questions.

1 Where will they have dinner?
2 Can you spell the name? Is it difficult?
3 At what time will they meet?
4 What is the number that Richard gives Tessa?

Developing language

Grammar: *going to*

1

Study the examples and answer the questions about them.

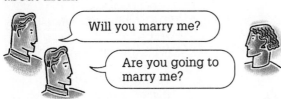

> Will you marry me?

> Are you going to marry me?

- Which example means, 'Do you plan to marry me?'
- What do you think the other example means?

2

Say it with *going to*.

Example: What do you plan to do this evening?

> What are you going to do this evening?

1 What do you plan to do tomorrow evening?
2 What do you plan to do next weekend?
3 Do you plan to marry my daughter?
4 When do you plan to marry her?
5 Do you intend to pay me the money you owe me?
6 When do you intend to pay me?
7 Does your company plan to bring out any new products soon?
8 Where do you plan to be this time tomorrow?

3 *Groupwork*

1 Find out about other people's plans in your class for
  a) tomorrow evening
  b) after this lesson
  c) this weekend
2 Now talk about your plans. Have you got any?

 See Grammar Summary 23, page 86.

Vocabulary: money

4

Which words have a connection with money? Put them in the money column. Put the other words in the second column and give that column a name.

- cheque • cash • clock • period • pay
- earn • spend • finance • capital • profit
- loss • budget • schedule • minute
- second • coin • hour

1 MONEY	2 _____
cheque	

Vocabulary: *make or do*

5

Which of these things can you *make*? Which can you *do*?

- a mistake • a profit • a loss
- a lot of money • plans for the future
- a job • a telephone call • your best
- coffee • tea • homework
- a test • an exercise like this

Pronunciation: /əʊ/ m**o**ment or /ɒ/ m**o**dern

6

a) When is the sound different?

1 pr**o**blem pr**o**duct pr**o**fit pr**o**gramme
2 pr**o**duct pr**o**gramme kn**ow** g**o**
3 cl**o**ck m**o**dern m**o**ment pr**o**duct
4 p**o**ssible pr**o**fit cl**o**ck m**o**ment
5 m**o**ment pr**o**gramme d**o**ctor s**o**

b) Listen and check.

Sales rise, profits fall

Look again at the title 'Sales rise, profits fall'. What is strange about it?

Reading

1

This is an article from an American business magazine.

Profits Down at Bradford Soft

Profits fell more than 40% at Bradford Soft last year, but according to its director, Dell Bradford, 'There's nothing to worry about.'

Bradford, 30, started the company seven years ago. Profits rose in the first three years, fell in the fourth, and then increased again in the next two.

'We're developing new software that will tell drivers about mechanical problems with their cars before they become serious. It's expensive to do this, and that's why sales were up but profits were down last year,' Bradford said yesterday.

'It's a good idea, but cars need good computers for that kind of software and most cars on the road today don't have them,' said George Tavrides, 42, who was Bradford's Sales Director for the first five years of the company's life and then

Bradford thinks ahead

quit after an argument with Bradford.

Dell Bradford didn't agree with Tavrides then and he doesn't agree with him now.

'In this business, the companies that do well are the ones that think ahead. That's what I'm doing.'

1

Are these explanations right or wrong?

1 Directors never worry when profits *fall*.
2 They often smile when profits *rise*.
3 When people *quit*, they leave a job.
4 People *argue* only when they *agree*.
5 *Think ahead* means 'plan for the future'.

2

Answer these questions.

1 Let's say that Bradford Soft made a profit of a million dollars two years ago. What was their profit last year?
2 Talk about the good and the bad years for Bradford. Say what was good or bad about them.
3 Do you think Tavrides really thinks the new software is a good idea? Give reasons for your answer.
4 Find all the examples you can of the word *that* in the text. Then explain exactly what each example means.
   Example: '. . . new software *that* will . . .'
   – *That* here means 'new software'.

Writing

3

Write a paragraph about

- Bradford Soft's financial situation in the last seven years
- the company's plans

Exploring language

Grammar: *that/who/which*

1

Make one sentence out of two.

Example: Bradford Soft is a company. It makes good software.
– Bradford Soft is a company that makes good software.

1 Computers are machines. They do wonderful things.
2 Who was that young man? He was here a minute ago.
3 Can you think of a phrase? It means the same thing as 'plan for the future'.
4 America is a big country. It has a lot of problems.
5 Who is that woman? She's standing near the door.

2

Study the examples. What's the rule?

1 Some of the people *who* work here have good ideas.
2 Some of the people *that* work here have good ideas.
3 Only a few of the products *which* come out every year really make a profit.
4 Only a few of the products *that* come out every year really make a profit.

- One of these rules is incorrect. Which one?

  - You can use either *who* or *that* for people.
  - You can use either *which* or *that* for things.
  - You can use *that* only for things and not for people.
  - You can use *which* for things but not for people.

- Now do exercise 1 again, but this time use *who* or *which* but not *that*. What is the reason for doing the exercise a second time?

> See Grammar Summary 28, page 88.

Vocabulary: *up* ↑ or *down* ↓

3

Put the words below in two groups:
Group 1 = up, Group 2 = down.

- fall • rise • increase • reduce • lower
- raise

4 *What about you?*

Questionnaire

1 Do you think prices will rise or fall in the next six months?
2 Which of the following things do you often spend money on?
   - entertainment • clothes • travel
   - books and magazines • tobacco • food
3 Which of the things above would you like to increase your spending on?
4 What would you like to reduce your spending on?
5 Which statement do you agree with?
   a) Taxes are too high; the Government should reduce them.
   b) Taxes are not high enough; the Government should increase them.

5

Complete the sentences.

rise or *raise*
1 Will the Government ____ our taxes?
2 Will taxes ____ again?

fall or *reduce*
3 Temperatures usually ____ in winter.
4 Can you ____ the temperature a little?

fall or *lower*
5 We think profits will ____ next year.
6 We plan to ____ our prices.

Can you use *increase* in both sentences?

7 We are going to ____ your salary.
8 Your salary is going to ____ .

Pronunciation: /ʃ/ sh

6

a) Which words have the /ʃ/ sound?

1 mechanic   machine
2 champagne   China
3 educate   education
4 direct   direction
5 act   action
6 information   position

b) Now listen and check.

Conversation 📼

Paula Silverman, of Metro Radio, is interviewing Tessa Saunders.

PAULA: Hello. I'm Paula Silverman, and welcome to Media World. We're delighted to have Tessa Saunders with us today from Knight and Day Advertising. Well, first of all, how long have you been working in advertising, Tessa?

TESSA: For five years.

PAULA: Could you tell us about your present job?

TESSA: Well, I'm an account executive. I work very closely with the client. We make decisions about the best advertising strategy for a product. I also work closely with the people who write the advertisements – the copywriters.

PAULA: And how long have you been doing that? Working as an account executive, I mean.

TESSA: For about three years.

PAULA: I have the impression that people don't last very long in advertising – that it's a good business to be in when you're young but not when you're older. Do you agree?

TESSA: Well, it is true that there are a lot of people below the age of thirty in advertising, and many of them earn very good salaries. But there are also a lot of older people in it, too.

PAULA: But isn't it much easier to lose a good job in your business than it is to get one?

TESSA: It isn't as safe as a job in a bank, if that's what you mean.

Before you begin

Can you explain the difference in the meaning of these two examples?

> She worked here for two years.

> She has been working here for two years.

1

Answer the questions.

1 When did Tessa get her first job in advertising?
2 How long ago did she become an account executive?
3 What does an account executive do?
4 What do you think Paula means when she says *you* in *when you're young but not when you're older*?
5 Does Tessa agree completely with Paula when she says that advertising isn't a good business to be in when you're older?

Listening 📼

2

Listen to the complete interview. Then answer the questions.

1 Do you think Tessa is happy with her job?
2 Give at least two reasons for your answer to question 1.
3 What are the things you think she doesn't like very much about her job?

Developing language

Grammar: Present Perfect Progressive

1 *What about you?*

1 Where do you live now?
2 How long have you been living there?
3 How long have you been learning English?
4 What is the name of your teacher?
5 How long has your teacher been teaching you English?
6 Do you do any of these things?
 • smoke • work in an office/a factory
 • go to school • drive • play a sport
 • play a musical instrument
7 Look back at all the things you answered 'Yes' to in question 6. Now say how long you've been doing these things.

2

What's the difference?

1 How long did Tessa live in Spain?

2 How long has Tessa been living in Spain?

• Tessa doesn't live in Spain any more. Which question is correct?
• Tessa lives in London now. Can you change one of the questions so that it is correct?

3

Complete these questions.

1 How long ___ you been waiting?
2 How long ___ it been raining?
3 How long have you ___ doing this job?
4 How long have you been ___ English?
5 How long ___ we been using this book?
6 How long ___ Paula been working for Metro Radio?

 See Grammar Summary 29, page 88.

Vocabulary: verbs and nouns

4
Complete the table.

	Verb	Noun
1	invite	invitation
2	discuss	?
3	?	decision
4	suggest	?
5	?	advice
6	know	?
7	?	product
8	lose	?
9	?	flight

5

Use the words in the table in exercise 4 to complete these sentences.

1 I'd like to ___ you to my party tomorrow.
2 I'd like to ___ a problem with you, please.
3 In this job a ___ of French and at least one other foreign language is necessary.
4 British Airways ___ 003 to Hong Kong is ready to depart.
5 Well, now you know what my problem is, what would you ___ me to do?
6 That's a good idea – a very useful ___ .
7 In some years we make a profit, but in other years we make a ___ . That's business.
8 Both products are very good. It's difficult to ___ which to buy.
9 We plan to begin selling the new ___ next month.

Pronunciation: verbs and nouns 📼

6

a) Say the words. Is the sound the same or different?

1 produce product
2 discuss discussion
3 advertise advertisement
4 invite invitation
5 know knowledge

b) Now listen and check.

A letter of application

Reading

Tessa'a boss, Richard Knight, received this letter not long ago.

```
                                        12 Morley Gardens
                                        LONDON SE3 1OS
    Richard Knight                      tel 071 459 8996
    Director
    Knight and Day
    33 Blake Street
    LONDON WC2 MX6


    28 March

    Dear Mr Knight

    I am writing to you on the recommendation of
    Olga Stavitska, who, as you know, is one of
    the directors of New Era Advertising here in
    London.

    I worked as a copywriter at New Era for
    three years. Immediately after that I spent
    two years at the Rodney Morris agency in New
    York, where I worked on a number of important
    projects. I was there until the end of last
    year.

    I have been back in England for six weeks
    and am looking for a job here. There are no
    positions available at the moment at New Era
    and this is why Olga advised me to contact you.

    I enclose references from all my previous
    employers, including New Era and Rodney Morris.
    I can come for an interview at any time that is
    convenient for you and look forward to your
    reply.

    Yours sincerely
    Brian O'Hara
    Brian O'Hara
```

1

Answer the questions.

1 Who gave Brian the idea of writing to Richard?
2 Where did Brian work before he went to America?
3 What did he do in America?
4 When did he come back?
5 Why didn't he go back to his old job at New Era Advertising?
6 Was there something else with the letter besides what you see here?

2 *Groupwork*

Here are four jobs you can apply for with Knight and Day. Find out which one people in your group are most interested in, and why.

- sales director
- receptionist
- trainee copywriter
- managing director

Writing

3

Write a short letter of application like the one above for one of the jobs in exercise 2.

Exploring language

Grammar: *some/any*

1

Discuss the difference.

1 Someone can do this job.

2 Anyone can do this job.

3 I'll come and see you sometime.

4 I'll come and see you any time.

- Find sentences above that mean these things.

a) Tell me when you want to see me, and I will come.

b) There is a person who can do this job, but I'm not saying this person's name.

c) This job is very easy. Even a child or a very stupid person can do it.

d) I'll come and see you, but I'm not saying exactly when.

2

In three of the sentences below *any* means 'no quantity at all'. But in three sentences the meaning is different. Which three?

1 I didn't do any work today.

2 I really don't want any wine.

3 Any bus that stops here will take you to Oxford Street.

4 Any child can learn this.

5 Don't give the police any information.

6 If you have any information about this, please tell us immediately.

3

Don't forget the basic meaning of *some* and *any*.

1 I'm very hungry. I didn't have ____ breakfast or lunch today.

2 Drink ____ of this. But not too much!

3 I'd like ____ information about the trains to London, please.

4 There isn't ____ paper in the photocopier.

5 Could you get ____ paper for the photocopier, please?

6 I need ____ money – not a lot; just a little.

7 I'm sorry, but I haven't got ____ money.

8 I didn't get ____ sleep at all last night.

 See Grammar Summary 26–27, page 87.

Vocabulary: words people confuse

Study the dictionary definitions.

4

rec-om-mend /ˌrekəˈmend/ *v* to say that someone or something is very good

ad-vise /ədˈvaɪz/ *v* to tell someone what you think they should do

en-close /ɪnˈkləʊz/ *v* to put something inside an envelope with a letter

in-clude /ɪnˈkluːd/ *v* to have or contain something as a part of a whole

em-ploy-er /ɪmˈplɔɪərʳ/ *n* a person or group that pays people to work for them

em-ploy-ee /ɪmˈplɔɪ-iː/ *n* a person who works for someone else

look for /lʊk fɔːr, fəʳ/ *phr v* to try to find someone or something

look at /lʊk æt, ət/ *phr v* to watch someone or something

Now choose the right word.

recommend or *advise*

1 Can you ____ a good wine to go with the fish?

2 I have a problem. Can you ____ me what to do?

enclose or *include*

3 All our prices ____ service and tax.

4 I ____ a stamped addressed envelope for your reply.

employer or *employee*

5 John was a very good ____. He was never late and always worked very hard.

6 If you would like further information about me, please contact my ____.

looking for or *looking at*

7 Why are you ____ that woman over there? Do you know her?

8 I'm ____ my money. I can't find it.

Pronunciation: *some*

5

a) **Listen to these sentences and repeat them. Can you hear a difference in the sound of *some*?**

1 There are some people outside.

2 I'd like some advice.

3 Only some people know about this. Not very many.

4 Some advice is good and some advice is bad.

b) **Now say these sentences, too. Is the sound of *some* always the same?**

1 I'd like some tea, please.

2 I like some films, but not all of them.

3 There are some words here I don't understand.

4 I understand some of these words, but not all of them.

15 The usual question

Before you begin

1 Have you ever worked in a hotel?
2 Have you ever told a lie?
3 Have you ever heard the word *ever* before?

Conversation

Roger Mitchum is having dinner with Anne Heller. She's looking for a job in San Francisco.

ROGER: You look worried.
ANNE: I am.
ROGER: Why?
ANNE: Well, I'm going to have an interview tomorrow, and I don't know what to say when they ask me the usual question.
ROGER: What question is that?
ANNE: 'Have you ever done this kind of work before?' You see, this company designs hotels, but all my experience has been in restaurant design.
ROGER: Yes, I know. But don't tell them that.
ANNE: Do you mean I should tell them a lie? Say that I have had some experience in designing hotels?
ROGER: No, of course not.
ANNE: Well, what should I say then?
ROGER: Say, 'No, I've never done that kind of thing before, but I have done things that are similar.'
ANNE: But that's not . . .
ROGER: Isn't there anything similar about designing restaurants and designing hotels?
ANNE: Well, the two things aren't completely different. I mean, hotels usually include restaurants.
ROGER: You see! There are things in your previous experience that can help you to get the job.
ANNE: Hmm. Perhaps you're right.

1

Answer the questions.

1 What is the question that Anne is worried about?
2 Why is she worried about it?
3 What does Roger think she should talk about at the interview?
4 Is this good advice? Give reasons.

Listening

2

Listen to the complete conversation. Then answer these questions.

1 Who asked these questions?

- *Would you like to talk about it?*
- *You mean you don't like him?*
- *What do you think you're going to do now?*

2 Can you remember the answers? Can you repeat them now?

Developing language

Grammar: Present Perfect Simple

1 Groupwork

Does *ever* mean a, b or c in the questions below?

a) at a definite, exact time in the past
b) at any time in the past
c) not very long ago in the past, perhaps in the last month or so

1 Have you ever studied a foreign language before?
2 Have you ever read an English book or newspaper?
3 Have you ever done something you were sorry about later?
4 Have you ever told a lie?
5 Have you ever written a letter of application?
6 Have you ever driven a very fast car?
7 Have you ever seen a famous person?
8 Have you ever asked any of these questions before?

• Now ask other people the eight questions. Get answers.

2

Look again at the questions in exercise 1. For all the questions that got the answer 'Yes', ask this question.

When did you . . . ?

The answer should always be in the past.

I did . . . last week.
I told . . . last month.
I saw . . . ago.

3

What are the missing words?

A: Have you ever ¹___ this kind of work before?
B: No, I ²___. But I ³___ done something very similar. When I ⁴___ in Japan, I ⁵___ for a company that specialises in restaurant design.
A: How long ⁶___ you work there?
B: For three years.
A: When ⁷___ you leave?
B: Last month.

 See Grammar Summary 30, page 89.

Vocabulary: *say* or *tell*

4

Which of these things can you *say*? Which can you *tell*?

• a lie • the truth • 'good morning' • 'hello'
• a story • 'goodbye' • a joke
• someone the way • 'thank you'

Pronunciation: stress

5

a) Listen to these conversations and then read them aloud.

A: Should I say I've done something I haven't done?
B: No, of course not.
A: Well, what should I say then?

A: Are you saying that I should lie?
B: No, of course not.
A: Well, what are you saying, then?

b) Read these conversations aloud, too. Which word do you think has the same stress as *should* and *are* in the conversations above?

A: Is Tessa in her office?
B: No, she isn't.
A: Well, where is she, then?

A: Did you go to work today?
B: No, I didn't.
A: Well, where did you go, then?

A: Would you like to see a film?
B: No.
A: Would you like to watch television?
B: No.
A: Well, what would you like to do, then?

Make a good impression

Reading

This is part of an article from an English magazine.

What are some questions I can ask them?

Find out as much as you can about the company before you go to the interview. What do they make or do? That is, what products do they manufacture? What services do they offer?

Then make a list of some of the questions your interviewers will probably ask you. When you have done this, think about the answers you can give.

At the same time, try to think of some questions you can ask them. Don't just answer only the questions they ask you. Always remember that it makes a better impression if you ask a few questions yourself.

What should I wear?

Choose something that makes you feel good and which you think will make the right impression on your interviewers. A bank or an insurance company will probably expect something formal and in a dark colour. But if you are applying for a job at an advertising agency, you can usually wear something more individual and unusual.

If you have been to an interview before and you didn't get the job, don't wear the same thing to the next interview. Perhaps you will connect it with failure and it will have the wrong psychological effect on you.

How long will it take to get there?

Never arrive at an interview late. At least a day before the interview, find out the best way to get there and how long it will take you. Always allow an extra fifteen minutes just in case there is a delay. Plan to get to the interview fifteen minutes early. This will not only make a good impression – it will also give you time to think about what you want to ask or say during the interview. For example, what about those questions you would like to ask about the company? This is the time to think about and remember them.

1 Answer the questions.

1 What is the difference between *products* and *services*? Give at least one example of each.
2 How can some clothes have *the wrong psychological effect on you*?
3 What does the writer say you should do before the interview? Why?
4 What should you do at the interview?
5 Explain why you should *always allow an extra fifteen minutes*.

2 *What about you?*

1 Do you think the article gives good advice?
2 What other advice about interviews would you give a young person?

3 *Groupwork*

Study this situation.

Anne is going for an interview tomorrow with an international construction company. The interview is at 11 am in San José, near San Francisco. Anne has never been to San José before.

- Now talk about these things.
  - what she should do before she goes to the interview
  - what she should wear
  - the questions she should ask

Exploring language

Grammar: three verb forms

1

Study the three forms of each verb. Which form (1, 2 or 3) should you use with *have* or *has*?

1	2	3
do/does see/sees drive/drives	did saw drove	done seen driven

2

Which of the columns above should these verb forms go in? Column 1, 2 or 3?

went	gone	go/goes
eat/eats	ate	eaten
known	knew	know/knows
was/were	is/are/am	been
gave	given	give/gives
take/takes	taken	took

3

What's the correct form?

Example: Have you (do) this kind of work before?
– done

1 Have you (see) any good films?
2 I (see) a very good film last week.
3 Have you ever (be) to the United States?
4 I (be) in San Francisco a few weeks ago.
5 I (write) three letters of application yesterday.
6 Have you (write) this many letters of application before?
7 Can you help the new secretary? She has never (do) this kind of work before.
8 I (do) a lot of work yesterday.
9 Have you ever (drive) a sports car?
10 When I was younger, I (drive) a Ferrari. Now I (drive) a Ford.

☞ See Grammar Summary 31, page 89.

Vocabulary: make or do

4

***make/makes* or *do/does*?**
1 A: What do you ____?
B: I'm an engineer.
2 Boeing is a company that ____ aeroplanes.
3 Did you ____ all the exercises on page 21?
4 Did you ____ any mistakes?
5 It ____ a bad impression if you come to an interview late.
6 Can you ____ me a cup of coffee?
7 Don't ____ so much noise.
8 Our company ____ a lot of business with companies in other parts of the world.

Pronunciation: same or different

5

a) **When is the sound different?**

1 d**o**ne   **o**ne   s**u**n   g**o**ne
2 d**o**ne   ph**o**ne   al**o**ne   l**oa**n
3 f**ou**nd   sh**ou**ld   w**ou**ld   c**ou**ld
4 f**ou**nd   t**ow**n   c**ou**ntry   c**ou**nt

b) **Now listen and check.**

Writing

6

Write down at least three things you've never done before, but which you would like to do. This is what one student wrote.

I've never been to the United States before, but I'd like to go there very much.
I've never driven a very fast car before either, but I'd like to.
I've never learned to play the piano, but I'd like to.

1 How many of these cities have people in your class been to?
  • New York   • Sydney   • Toronto
2 Think of three more big cities. Find other students in your class who have been to them.
3 What do you think is the difference in meaning between these two questions?
  • Have you learned English yet?
  • Have you ever learned English?

Conversation 📼

Richard Knight and Tessa are in a restaurant in London. They are waiting for Richard's partner, Donald Day. Day is the director of the New York office of Knight and Day.

RICHARD: You've met Donald before, haven't you?
TESSA: Um, yes, when he was over here two years ago.
RICHARD: I thought so . . .
TESSA: Excuse me, Richard. But what exactly is all this about? You haven't told me yet.
RICHARD: What's it all about?
TESSA: Yes, Richard. You've never invited me to dinner before. So why now? What exactly do you want to talk to me about?
RICHARD: I'll let Donald explain that. He'll be here soon.
TESSA: But why can't you . . .
RICHARD: By the way, have you ever been to New York?
TESSA: Yes, I was there for a week about five years ago.
RICHARD: What did you think of it?
TESSA: It's a very interesting city.
RICHARD: Do you think you'd like to live there?
TESSA: I'm not sure. I've never really thought about it. Why?
RICHARD: As I said, I think Donald should explain that. Look! He's just got out of that taxi. He'll tell you . . .

1

Complete the questions.

1 ___ Tessa met Donald before?
2 When ___ she meet him?
3 ___ Tessa ever been to dinner with Richard before?
4 ___ she ever been to New York?
5 When ___ she there?
6 ___ she like to live there?

• Now talk about the answers.

2 *What about you?*

1 What do you know about New York?
2 Do you think you would like to live there? Why or why not?

Listening 📼

3

Listen to the complete conversation. Then answer these questions.

1 What is the most important thing that Donald tells Tessa?
2 What important question does Richard ask?
3 What is Tessa's answer?

Developing language

Grammar: past participles

1

Study the table.

Regular			Irregular		
work		worked	see		seen
watch	*has*	watched	do	*has*	done
like	*have*	liked	take	*have*	taken
advise		advised	tell		told

- Which of these examples are regular? Which are irregular?

1 Tessa *has met* Donald before.
2 Tessa *has talked* to Donald before.
3 *Have* you ever *played* tennis?
4 *Have* you *brought* your tennis shoes with you?
5 *Has* the train *arrived* yet?
6 *Has* the train *come* yet?
7 *Have* you *eaten* yet?
8 *Have* you *finished* eating yet?

2

Complete the table.

1	do/does	did	done
2	tell/tells	told	?
3	go/goes	went	?
4	write/writes	wrote	?
5	think/thinks	thought	?
6	look/looks	looked	?
7	ask/asks	asked	?
8	say/says	said	?
9	buy/buys	bought	?
10	make/makes	made	?
11	have/has	had	?
12	sell/sells	sold	?

☞ See Grammar Summary 31, page 89.

Grammar: question tags

3

Study these two ways of asking questions.

> You've done this before, haven't you?

> Have you done this before?

- Ask these questions in the same way as *Have you done this before*?

1 This is the last unit of the book, isn't it?
2 You can understand this, can't you?
3 Tessa lives in London, doesn't she?
4 You did this yesterday, didn't you?
5 Anne likes Roger, doesn't she?
6 She met him on a plane, didn't she?
7 She lived in Tokyo before, didn't she?
8 You've been to Tokyo, haven't you?
9 This exercise was easy, wasn't it?

Vocabulary: meet, introduce and know

4

meet, introduce or know?

1 Do you ____ the meaning of these words?
2 Do you always say 'How do you do?' when you first ____ a person?
3 Please ____ me to your friend.
4 I'd like to discuss something with you. When can we ____?
5 Does Tessa ____ Donald very well?
6 When did Richard ____ her to him?

5

Which of the words or phrases below can we use *I know* with? All of them, or only some?

- a person   • something about a person
- a city or country   • how to do something
- what to do or say in a certain situation
- the answer to a question

- Now make different examples of your own with *know*.

Example: – Do you know my friend, Peter?

An offer she can't refuse?

Reading

This is a letter from Tessa to her old friend, Roger Mitchum.

Dear Roger,

I haven't heard from you for a long time now. It must be almost three months. I hope you're all right and still enjoying life in San Francisco.

As for myself, I've been very busy since I last spoke to you (I think you were in Japan at the time, and phoned me. Do you remember?) One of the reasons I am writing to you now is to ask you for some advice. Let me explain the situation.

I have been at Knight and Day for four years now. Perhaps you remember that Richard Knight is the director of the London office and his partner, Donald Day, is the Director of the New York office. Well, yesterday evening, over dinner, they offered me a job in the New York office.

I didn't accept the job immediately. I told them I would like to think about it, and they gave me a week or so to make up my mind.

One reason I am hesitating is that I am not sure if I would like to live in New York. I know it is an exciting and fascinating city, but it also seems a very difficult place to live in. At least that was the impression I had when I was there for a week five years ago.

I am also a little worried about the financial side of the offer. My salary would be better (about $5,000 more than I am earning now). However, do you think the cost of living in New York or San Francisco is higher than here in London? I know the prices of some things are lower in America, but what about rents?

Are you happier in the United States than you were here? What do you think are the advantages of living there when compared with life in England? I really would value your opinion.

I look forward to hearing from you.

Love,
Tessa.

1

Discuss the questions.

1 What happened when Tessa had dinner with Richard Knight and Donald Day?
2 What is one reason she didn't accept immediately?
3 What other reason has she got for hesitating?
4 Why do you think she is writing to Roger about this?
5 What does she want Roger to tell her in his answer?

2 *What about you?*

1 What do you think are some of the advantages of living and working in a foreign country?
2 Can you think of any disadvantages of living abroad?

3 *Roleplay*

You work for a large international company. Your boss has just offered you a job in the new Moscow office. The main advantage of taking the job is a salary that is $5,000 higher than what you are earning now. Your boss will also give you a free return ticket home and an extra week's holiday once a year.

You like living where you do now. You have many friends and also a family here. In groups discuss:

- the disadvantages of taking the job
- what you should ask for (more money, etc) before you take the job
- exactly what you can say to your boss when you ask for these things

Now, with someone else, roleplay the situation between you and your boss.

Writing

4

Write a letter to a friend, telling him/her what you decided in the roleplay – to take the job, or not to take it.

Exploring language

Grammar: *seem*

1

What's the difference?

1 This is a good offer.
This seems to be a good offer.
2 You don't understand.
You don't seem to understand.
3 My boss likes my work.
My boss seems to like my work.

- In each pair of sentences, which means 'This is my impression. Perhaps I am wrong but I think I am probably right'?

2

***seem* or *seems*?**

1 Tessa ____ to like her job very much.
2 You ____ worried today. What's wrong?
3 English people sometimes ____ to be a little arrogant.
4 Roger sometimes ____ to be a little arrogant.
5 Does this exercise ____ useful?
6 Do these exercises ____ useful?
7 Tessa doesn't ____ very happy today.
8 You don't ____ very happy today.

3

Change the sentences so that they mean, 'This is my impression. Perhaps I am wrong, but I think I am probably right.'

1 Tessa likes her job.
2 Roger doesn't like his job.
3 He is very interested in Anne.
4 This restaurant is a good place to eat.
5 That pub is closed.
6 You don't like this exercise.
7 You know a lot of English.
8 You have an excellent vocabulary.

Vocabulary: *price, cost* and *value*

4

Study the examples.
- You can usually see the *price* of a book on the front or back cover.
- The *cost* of living is going up.
- Sometimes the *price* of something is above or below its true *value*.

- Now complete the sentences. Use *price*, *cost* or *value*.

1 Excuse me, what is the ____ of these jeans? I can't see it anywhere.
2 If we want to increase our profits, we have to keep our ____s down.
3 What is the ____ of great literature or music? I mean, why do you think these things are so important?
4 The ____ of the Gulf War was very high.
5 We have a very high opinion of the ____ of your work and cooperation.
6 What is the ____ of petrol in your country?

Pronunciation: weak forms 🔲

5

a) Listen to these sentences and then repeat them.

1 Has the film begun?
2 Yes, it has.
3 I don't know where Tessa is. I think she has gone home.
4 Have you eaten yet?
5 Yes, I have.
6 I'm not hungry. I have already eaten.
7 Excuse me. I think you have forgotten something.

b) Now can you answer these questions?

1 In which sentence could you write *'s* and not *has*?
2 In which sentences could you write *'ve* and not *have*?

Grammar Summary

1

Personal pronouns and possessives

1.1 Subject pronouns

Words like *I*, *you* and *she* are subject pronouns.

1 Can *I* help you?
2 Are *you* from London?
3 Tessa is English. *She* works in London.

1.2 Object pronouns

Words like *me*, *you* and *her* are object pronouns.

1 Can you help *me*?
2 Can I help *you*?
3 This is Tessa. Do you know *her*?

1.3 Possessive adjectives

Words like *my*, *your* and *her* are possessive adjectives.

1 'Is this *your* first name?'
   'No, it's *my* surname.'
2 Tessa comes from Liverpool, but *her* father comes from Bristol.

2

Verb *to be*

2.1 Affirmative form

I	*am*		England
She		from	Spain
He	*is*		Japan
It			Brazil
We		in	Argentina
You	*are*		Turkey
They			Russia

When we speak, we often use short forms.
I am = I'm
You are = You're
It is = It's

2.2 Question form

This is how we ask questions with the verb *to be*.

You *are* English.
Are you English?

She *is* from Spain.
Is she from Spain?

2.3 Negative form

We make negative sentences with *is*, *are* and *am*, with *not*.

I	*'m not*		Spanish
She			English
He	*isn't*		from Paris
We			hungry
They	*aren't*		tired

These are the short forms.
I am not = I'm not
He is not = He isn't
You are not = You aren't

3

Prepositions

Prepositions are words like *on*, *in* and *at*. They are very important in English. Here are fifteen of the most important.

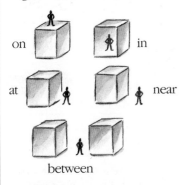

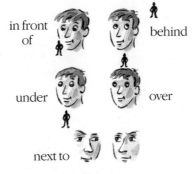

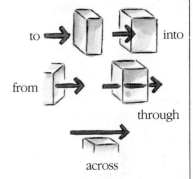

Examples

1 Your book is *on* the table.
2 What's *in* that box?
3 Who's that *at* the door?
4 There's a good pub *near* the office.
5 This is a secret, *between* you and me.

6 The teacher is standing *in front of* the class.
7 Who is standing *behind* you?
8 What's *under* the table?
9 We are flying *over* the Pacific.
10 Who is sitting *next to* you?

11 I'm going *to* London.
12 Come *into* my office.
13 I'm *from* Texas.
14 What can you see when you look *through* the window?
15 Walk *across* the street and turn left.

4

can

4.1 Affirmative form

I You He She We They	can	drive do it come now see you at 5

We use *can* in many ways in English.
'I can drive' really means 'I know how to drive.'
'I can do it' means 'I have the ability to do it.'
'I can see you at 5' means 'If you want to see me at 5, it is all right.'

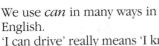

4.2 Question form

You *can* help me.
Can you help me?

He *can* drive.
Can he drive?

Put *Can* in front of the subject pronoun in questions.

Notice again that there are many meanings here. For example, 'Can the doctor see me at 5?' means 'I want to see the doctor at 5. Is that all right?'

4.3 Negative form

I We He She	can't cannot	help you do this see you now

This is the negative form. We write *cannot*, but we usually say *can't*.

We use *can* for all persons (*I*, *she*, *they*, etc.).
The verb (*help*, *do*, *come*, *see*) is always without *to*.

5

Plural nouns

5.1 Regular plurals

a car   two cars   a match   matches

The plural form of a noun is the form that means 'more than one'. Most plural forms in English are regular. We make regular plurals by putting an -s or an -es on the end of the noun.

5.2 Irregular plurals

There are a few (not many) nouns in English which have irregular plurals. Here are six important irregular plurals.

a *man*   men   a *woman*   women

a child   child*ren*   foot   feet

a person   people   a tooth   teeth

6

Quantity

6.1 *How much?*

How *much*	tea coffee money beer time	is there? have we got?

We use *much* with words like 'time', 'money', 'tea' and 'coffee'. These are mass words (see 6.3).

6.2 *How many?*

How *many*	people students books chairs bottles	are there? have you got?

We use *many* with the plural form of words. These are unit words (see 6.3).

6.3 Mass and unit words

MASS	UNIT
coffee rain money time music	cups of coffee metres of rain coins dollars symphonies

Mass words are for things we don't count or see separately. 'Money' is a mass word. We count money, of course, but when we count it, we count dollars, Deutschmarks and yen, etc. 'Time' is also a mass word. We don't really count time. We count minutes, hours, days and weeks.

Unit words are words for things we can count and see separately. 'Dollars', 'minutes', 'hours', 'cups of coffee', 'people' and 'books' are all unit words.

7

Demonstratives

7.1 *this* and *these*

here   here
this chair   *these* chairs

We use *this* with singular nouns and *these* with plurals. We use *this* and *these* with things that are here – things that are very near us when we speak.

7.2 *that* and *those*

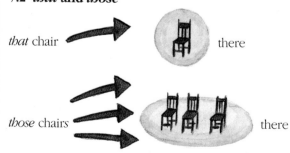

that chair   there

those chairs   there

When the thing or things are not very near – when they are there and not here, we say *that* (for singular nouns) and *those* (for plurals).

8

Present Simple

8.1 Affirmative form

I We You They	live work	
		here
He She	lives works	

We use the Present Simple to talk about things that are true in the present, but usually they are not happening when we speak. For example, if you are at a bus stop and you see the bus, you say, 'The bus is coming' and not 'The bus comes.'

Remember that with *He*, *She* and *It*, there is always an -*s* or an -*es* at the end of the verb.

8.2 Question form

You *live* here.
Do you *live* here?

She *lives* here.
Does she *live* here?

We use *Do* or *Does* in the question. But look at the main verb (*live, work*). We never put an -*s* or -*es* after the main verb in the question form.

8.3 Negative form

I We You They	don't	live here work here understand like this want it know
She He	doesn't	

Use *don't* or *doesn't* to make the negative.

Notice! There is no -*s* or -*es* at the end of the main verb (*live, work, understand*).

9

Present Progressive

9.1 Affirmative form

I	am	
She He It	is	going coming waiting leaving
You We They	are	

One of the important uses of the Present Progressive is to talk about something that is happening when we talk.

1 Look! The bus *is coming*!
2 Excuse me. You're *standing* on my foot!

Remember the weak forms.

I'*m* ... / She'*s* ... / We'*re* ... -ing.

9.2 Question form

It *is* raining.
Is it raining?

You *are* leaving.
Are you leaving?

We form questions in the Present Progressive in the same way we do with the verb *to be*.

9.3 Negative form

I	am		listening
It	is	not	coming watching
They	are		working

Put *not* between *am, is* or *are* and the -*ing* form of the verb (*listening, coming*).

Remember the weak forms. (I'*m not* ..., He *isn't* ..., We *aren't* ... -ing.)

9.4 Present Simple/Present Progressive

What do you do? and *What are you doing?* mean very different things.

> What *does* he *do*?
> He's the director of an advertising agency.
> What's he doing?
> He's *having* a shower.

Questions like *What do you do?* mean 'What's your job?'
You can also use the Present Progressive to talk about things you plan to do in the future.

> What *are* you do*ing* this evening?
> I'*m going* to a jazz concert tomorrow.
> We're leav*ing* in five minutes.

10

Wh -question words

Remember these words, too.

What ... ? name of thing
What do you do?
What's that?

Where ... ? place, location
Where do you live?
Where do you come from?

How ... ? in what way, number
How do you spell your name?
How old are you?

When ... ? time
When does the film start?

Why ... ? reason, cause
Why aren't you at work?

has/have got

11.1 Affirmative form

He She I You We They	*has* got *have*	a problem a good job some news a headache

The word *got* here has no real meaning. It is an 'empty' word, but we often use it with *have* in the present tense.

Remember the weak forms.

I*'ve* got . . .   She*'s* got . . .

This word is *has* not *is*.

11.2 Question form

You *have got* a car.
Have you *got* a car?

She *has got* a car.
Has she *got* a car?

When you are talking about possession, put *Have* or *Has* in front of the subject (*you, he, she*).

But remember that in American English people often say '*Do* you *have* a car?'

11.3 Negative form

haven't got

I He	have has	*not* got	a car

hasn't got

This is the negative form of only the 'possessive' meaning of *have*. There are other meanings of *have* (see Unit 3, Exploring Language, p 25).

some/any

12.1 *some*

I can see Play I need	*some*	people music money

The word *some* in English means 'a number or quantity of . . .'. We use it when we don't know or don't want to say the exact amount or number.

I don't understand *some* of these words.

I'd like *some* information.

12.2 *any*

I can't see I don't want I haven't got	*any*	people music money

In negative sentences *any* can mean 'none at all' or 'not even one'.

There isn't *any* film in the camera.
I didn't see *any* good films last month.

But it can also have another meaning.

Take *any* bus from here.
They all go to Victoria.

Here it means 'It isn't important which one.'

Frequency adverbs

100%	■ always
75%	■ usually
50%	■ often
25%	□ sometimes
0%	□ never

Words like *always, usually, often, sometimes* and *never* are called frequency adverbs. We use them when we talk about how often we do things.

Remember where they go in the sentence.

I We	*usually often never*	drive to work get up before 8

This is where we usually (not always) put frequency adverbs. Sometimes we put the word *sometimes* at the beginning.

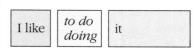

Sometimes I love you and *sometimes* I hate you.

would like

14.1 *I like/I'd like*

I'd like is a polite way of saying 'I want'. *I like* means 'I enjoy'.

Compare.

1 I *like* tea in the morning. (I like tea every morning.)
2 *I'd like* tea in the morning. (Please bring me some tea tomorrow morning.)

14.2 *I like . . .-ing/I'd like to . . .*

We can use two different verb forms after *like* or *likes*.

I like	*to do doing*	it

There is very little difference in meaning.

I like *to play* tennis.
I like *playing* tennis.

But with *would like*, use the full infinitive (*to do*).

Would you like *to go* to the cinema with me?

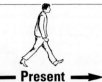

 15

Past, present and future

| Past | ← **Present** → | **Future** |

Past

work want + ed	did	
came	didn't go	
had	like live + d	
didn't like	went	
knew		

The past is behind you. When we talk about the past in English, we use special verb forms.

Yesterday I *worked* from 9 to 6.
What *did* you *do* yesterday?

Present

works wants	does
is coming comes	likes/ doesn't like
knows	lives
has got hasn't got	is going goes

You are in the present now. Remember that we have two present forms in English.

What *do* you *do*?
What *are* you *doing*?

(See sections 8 and 9.)

One is for habits. The other is for things that are happening now.

Future

is going to do
will do
will come
is going to have
will go
won't have

The future is in front of you. In English there are many ways of talking about the future. In this book you are going to learn two future forms. They are *will do* and *going to do*/won't do and isn't going to do.

16

Past Simple

16.1 Affirmative form of the verb *to be*

I He She It	*was*	last year
		here yesterday
		there in 1990
You We They	*were*	last week

Compare this with the present of *to be* (see section 2).

Question form of *to be*

You *were* here yesterday.
Were you here yesterday?

Tessa *was* away yesteday.
Was Tessa away yesterday?

Put *were* or *was* in front of the subject (*you*, *she*, etc.).

Negative form of *to be*

 I wasn*'t*.
You weren*'t*.

This is the form we use when we speak. The full written form is *was not* and *were not*.

16.2 Affirmative form of regular verbs

walk work play watch	+ *ed*	like hope use arrive + *d*

Regular past forms are verbs like *walk*, *work*, *like* and *hope*. We call them 'regular' because we put -*ed* or -*d* on the end. Compare these with irregular past forms (16.3).

Question form of regular verbs

Romeo *loved* Juliet.

Did Romeo *love* Juliet?

Negative form of regular verbs

They *lived* in Verona.

They *didn't live* in Pisa.

Use *did* (for all persons) and the plain infinitive (*like*, *work*; not *to like* or *to work*) in questions. Use *didn't* in the negative form.

16.3 Affirmative form of irregular verbs

Irregular verbs change in a number of ways. Here are just a few of them. Look at the complete list on page 90.

go(es)	*went*
grow(s)	*grew*
speak(s)	*spoke*
take(s)	*took*
know(s)	*knew*
do(es)	*did*

Question and negative forms of irregular verbs

She *went* to London.
Where *did* she *go*?

You *saw* a film.
What *did* you *see*?

We *went* to London.
We *didn't go* to Paris.

We *saw* 'Superman'.
We *didn't see* 'Batman'.

Always use the infinitive form (the same as the Present Simple without -*s* or -*es*) in the question and negative forms.

for/ago

17.1 two years *ago*

She lived in Spain two years *ago*.

SPAIN

one year
one year

Now

When we use *ago* we count the time between the present and when something happened in the past.

It's nine o'clock. Tessa came to work an hour ago (at eight).

She came to work an hour *ago*.

17.2 *for* two years

Now

She lived in Spain *for* two years.

This example doesn't tell us exactly when she lived in Spain. It tells us only how long she lived there.

She slept *for* six hours last night.

If Tessa went to bed at 1 o'clock and got up at 7 o'clock, we can say, 'She slept for six hours last night.'

Compare *for* and *ago*.

How long was Tessa at Cambridge?

For three years.

When did she leave Cambridge?

Seven years *ago*.

Comparatives

18.1 Use

Comparatives are words like *better*, *worse*, *warmer* and *colder*. We use them to compare two or more people or things.

Alex 20   Ruth 52

He is *younger* than she is.

Tokyo 32°C   London 18°C

It's *warmer* in Tokyo than in London.

18.2 Regular comparatives

Here are some examples of regular comparatives.

+ *r* or *er*

young	*younger*
old	*older*
tall	*taller*
short	*shorter*
late	*later*
hard	*harder*

Notice the change in spelling when the word ends in *y*.

earl happ + *y*	⇨	earl happ + *ier*

18.3 Irregular comparatives

There are a few irregular comparatives.

Mac

This computer is *good*.

Supermac

But this one is *better*.

The weather is *bad* today.

But yesterday it was *worse*.

18.4 -*er*/*more*

We make the comparative form of longer words like this.

ex-pen-sive	*more* expensive
im-por-tant	*more* important
in-te-lli-gent	*more* intelligent

For example, we say:

> A Mercedes is *more expensive* than a Ford.

> What's *more important*? Love or money?

18.5 *as/than*

Use *than* only with the comparative form of adjectives (*bigger than . . .* , *more important than . . .*).

Alex 20   Laura 20

He's *as* old *as* she is.

Alex 20   Ruth 52

He is young*er than* she is.

19

Superlatives

19.1 Use

Alex   Mary   Ruth
20   37   52

> Ruth is *the oldest*.

> Alex is *the youngest*.

Words like *the oldest*, *the youngest*, *the best* and *the most expensive* are called superlatives. We use them when we compare more than two things or people.

19.2 *-est/the most*

If the adjective (*good, cheap, expensive*) is more than two syllables (*ex-pen-sive*), we say *the most* and not *-est*.

£10,000

£300,000

£45,000

> The black one is *the most expensive* and *the most comfortable* car here.

19.3 Irregular superlatives

The adjectives *good* and *bad* have irregular superlative forms.

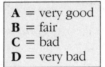

A =	very good
B =	fair
C =	bad
D =	very bad

A is *the best* mark you can get and D is *the worst*.

20

should

20.1 A modal verb

We call words like *should* modal verbs. Modal verbs are verbs that tell us about people's feelings about something. Compare these sentences.

1 Richard smokes cigars.
2 Tessa thinks he *shouldn't* smoke in the office.
3 'You *should* smoke that thing outside,' she said a few days ago.

Example 1 doesn't tell us anything about Tessa's feelings.

But examples 2 and 3 tell us that Tessa thinks it is wrong that Richard smokes cigars in the office.

20.2 Affirmative form

He She You	*should*	see a doctor leave now do it

Notice that we use *should* for all persons.

20.3 Question and negative forms

I *should* learn French.
Should I learn French?

When we ask questions with *should*, we simply change the position of *should* and the subject (*I, he, she*).

You should*n't* smoke here.
should not

We make the negative form in the same way we do with *can, is, has* or *have*.

21

could

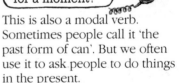
> *Could* you come to my office for a moment?

This is also a modal verb. Sometimes people call it 'the past form of can'. But we often use it to ask people to do things in the present.

We use the same form of the word with all persons.

I/We She/He They You	*can should could*	do it come leave start finish

We use *could* with the plain infinitive – exactly the same form we use with *can* and *should*.

Can you *help* me?
Should I *see* a doctor?
Could you *come* later?

22

will

22.1 Affirmative form

Tomorrow *will* be a warm and sunny day.

We often use *will* to make predicitons. An example of a prediction is the weather report on the radio.

We also use *will* to make promises.

I'll always love you.

The short form is *'ll*. This is the form people usually use when they speak.

| I She You | will | ⇨ | I She You | 'll |

22.2 Question and negative forms

We ask questions in the same way we do with *can* and *should*.

It *will* rain tomorrow.
Will it rain tomorrow?

The negative form is *will not* or *won't*.

Listen to this! You *won't* believe it but . . .

23

going to

23.1 Affirmative form

| I She We | *am* *is* *are* | *going to* | be late leave see a film have a party |

Going to is another important future form in English. We often use it when we can see something now that tells us something about the future. For example, you see dark clouds in the sky and say, 'It's going to rain.'

Look! It's *going to* rain.

We also use *going to* to talk about plans and intentions.

I'm *going to* be a millionaire when I'm older. I'm *going to* have a big . . .

23.2 Question and negative forms

It *is* going to rain.
Is it going to rain?

You *are* going to do it.
Are you going to do it?

| I He We | 'm not isn't aren't | going to . . . |

Notice again the question form. We call this 'inversion' – that is, we change the position of words.

23.3 *will/going to*

Use *will* when you promise or offer to do something.

I'll answer it.

You can also use *will* when you ask someone to do something.

Will you answer it, please?

But when you want to talk or ask about intentions, use *going to*.

What are you going to do?

24

have to

24.1 Affirmative form

He *has to* work late this evening. He *has to* finish a report.

This is one of the ways in English we can say, 'It is necessary to do this.'

24.2 Question form

I *have to* do it.
Do you *have to* do it?

He *has to* do it.
Does he *have to* do it?

Ask questions with *Do* or *Does* and the plain infinitive (*have*).

Answer it!
Do I have to?

24.3 Negative form

> You *don't have to* answer it. It isn't important.

This means 'It isn't necessary to do it.'

Tessa *doesn't have to* work on Sunday, but she often does. You *don't have to* explain this. I already understand it.

Use *don't have* or *doesn't have* + the full infinitive (*to go, to work, to come*).

25

Adjectives and adverbs

Compare the two sentences.

1 Your English is very *good*.
2 You speak English very *well*.

The word *good* is an adjective. We use adjectives with nouns (your *English*, the *film*, this *book*) and the verb *to be* (*is, are, am, was, were*).
The word *well* is an adverb. We use adverbs with verbs (*speak, do, play, talk, read*).
Most adverbs have *-ly* on the end.

clear*ly* bad*ly* quick*ly* stupid*ly*

Some adverbs, however, are irregular. For example, *well* in example 2 above. Here are some more.

1 He's a fast driver.
  He drives very *fast*.
2 She's a hard worker.
  She works *hard*.
3 Your English is better than it was.
  You speak English *better* than you did before.
4 Fred is a worse driver than Mary.
  Fred drives *worse* than Mary does.

Notice that *fast*, *hard*, *better*, and *worse* do not change in form at all. The comparative forms of *fast* and *hard* do not change, either.

> Work *harder*! Work *faster*! Then you can live *better* and not *worse* than you do now!

26

something/anything/nothing

First, be sure you understand these examples.

There's *something* in this glass. Do you know what it is?

There isn't *anything* in this glass. It's empty.

This glass is empty, too. There's *nothing* in it.

Use *something* when you don't know or don't want to say exactly what the thing is. Don't use it in negative sentences.

Use *anything* in negative sentences. In negative sentences it means the same as *nothing*.

Nothing is a negative word. It means *not anything*. Don't use it with *not* in a sentence. The idea of *not* is already in the word.

27

someone/anyone

> *Someone* wants to talk to you.

> I don't want to see or talk to *anyone* today. I'm too busy.

Use *someone* or *somebody* when you don't know or don't want to say the name of the person you are talking about.

In negative sentences, when you mean 'not one person' or 'no-one', use *anyone* or *anybody*.

You can use *anyone* or *anybody* in other ways, as well.

> Ask *anyone*. They will all give you the same answer.

Here, it means 'It doesn't matter which person you ask.' In other words, *any* here has the same meaning that *any* has in sentences like 'Any bus will take you to Victoria Station.' (See 12.2.)

> Do you know *anyone* here?

> Can *anybody* here help me? I need some information.

In these examples, the meaning is similar. Again, *anybody* or *anyone* means 'It isn't important who.'

28

that/who/which

You can use the word *that* to make one sentence out of two.

I work for a company.
It makes software.

> I work for a company *that* makes software.

Who was that man?
He was here a minute ago.

> Who was the man *that* was here a minute ago?

You can also use the words *who* and *which* in this way. But there are things you have to remember.

Use *who* only for people, or sometimes animals with names.

All the people *who* work with Tessa like her.
Fido is a small dog with one ear *who* lives with an old woman.

You can also use *which*, but only for things or animals.

Birds are animals *which* fly. Love, music and money are three of the things *which* make life interesting.

You can use *that* for things, people and animals.

Where are those things *that* were on the table?
Do you remember the man and woman *that* came in here yesterday at about five o'clock?

29

Present Perfect Progressive

29.1 Affirmative form

have
has   been . . . *-ing*

Past   Present

You can use the Present Perfect Progressive in a number of ways. One of the most important is when you are asking or talking about something that is happening now but which began in the past.

> How long *have* you *been* waiting?

The woman began waiting for the bus in the past. She is still doing it.

> I've been standing here for an hour.

Remember! All these examples are about something that started in the past but which is still going on.

Past   Present

29.2 Present Perfect Progressive/Past Simple

Tessa lived in Spain for a year.

Past

This is over and finished. Tessa doesn't live in Spain any more.

Tessa has been living in London for four years.

Past   Present

This started in the past, but it is still going on. Tessa is living in London now.

29.3 Present Perfect Progressive/Present

When you are talking about something that began in the past and is still going on, don't use the Present Simple or Progressive. A question like

> How long *are* you *staying* here?

means the same as 'How long are you going to stay here?' But a question like

> How long *have* you *been staying* here?

means the same as 'When did you come here? How long ago was that?' *How long* here begins in the past and comes into the present.

Present Perfect Simple

Have you *done* it before?

Past   Present

When you ask a question like this, you are looking from the present back to the past. This is very similar to another question.

Have you *ever* done it?

Past   Present

The word *ever* here means 'at any time in your life'.

> Have you *ever* been to Paris?

> Yes, I have.

> Have you been here *before*?

> No. This is my first visit.

Past participles

31.1 Regular and irregular verbs

We use a special form of the verb in the Present Perfect. We call it the 'past participle'.

Have you ever	done been seen had	. . .?

I *lived* in Paris for three months in 1991.
Have you ever *lived* in Paris?

Compare this with the irregular forms of the Past Simple and past participle.

We *did* this last week.
Have you ever *done* this before?

I *saw* that film last month.
Have you *seen* this film before?

See section 32 for a list of the most important irregular verbs in this book.

31.2 Past Simple/past participle

The Past Simple form and the past participle are the same in regular verbs.

ask like use	asked liked used	asked liked used

But the Past Simple form and the past participle are often different in irregular verbs.

do see take	did saw took	done seen taken

32

Important irregular verbs

The first form of the verb (*be*) is the infinitive form.
I have to *be* in London tomorrow.

The second form is the past form.
I *was* in London yesterday. Where *were* you?

The third form is the form of the verb we use with the Present Perfect – the past participle.
Have you *been* here before?

Infinitive	Past	Past Participle
be	was, were	been
become	became	become
break	broke	broken
bring	brought	brought
build	built	built
buy	bought	bought
catch	caught	caught
come	came	come
do	did	done
drink	drank	drunk
drive	drove	driven
eat	ate	eaten
fall	fell	fallen
feel	felt	felt
find	found	found
fly	flew	flown
get	got	got
give	gave	given
go	went	gone
grow	grew	grown
have	had	had
hear	heard	heard
hold	held	held
know	knew	known
learn	learnt	learnt
leave	left	left
lend	lent	lent
lose	lost	lost
make	made	made
mean	meant	meant
pay	paid	paid
read	read	read
rise	rose	risen
say	said	said
sell	sold	sold
send	sent	sent
shut	shut	shut
sing	sang	sung
sleep	slept	slept
speak	spoke	spoken
spell	spelt	spelt
spend	spent	spent
stand	stood	stood
swim	swam	swum
take	took	taken
teach	taught	taught
think	thought	thought
throw	threw	thrown
understand	understood	understood
wear	wore	worn
win	won	won
write	wrote	written

Pronunciation Table

CONSONANTS		VOWELS	
Symbol	Key Word	Symbol	Key Word
p	**p**ack	e	b**e**d
b	**b**ack	æ	b**a**d
t	**t**ie	iː	sh**ee**p
d	**d**ie	ɪ	sh**i**p
k	**c**lass	ɑː	c**a**lm
g	**g**lass	ɒ	p**o**t
		ɔː	c**au**ght, h**or**se
tʃ	**ch**ur**ch**	ʊ	p**u**t
dʒ	**j**u**dg**e	uː	b**oo**t
		ʌ	c**u**t
f	**f**ew	ɜː	b**ir**d
v	**v**iew	ə	bett**er**
θ	**th**row		
ð	**th**ough	eɪ	m**a**ke
s	**s**oon	əʊ	b**oa**t
z	**z**oo	aɪ	b**i**te
ʃ	**sh**oe	aʊ	n**ow**
ʒ	mea**s**ure	ɔɪ	b**oy**
		ɪə	h**ere**
m	su**m**	eə	h**air**
n	su**n**	ʊə	p**oor**
ŋ	su**ng**		
h	**h**ot	eɪə	pl**ayer**
l	**l**ot	əʊə	l**ower**
r	**r**od	ɔɪə	empl**oyer**
j	**y**et	aɪə	t**ire**
w	**w**et	aʊə	fl**ower**

Numbers

1	one	1st	first
2	two	2nd	second
3	three	3rd	third
4	four	4th	fourth
5	five	5th	fifth
6	six	6th	sixth
7	seven	7th	seventh
8	eight	8th	eighth
9	nine	9th	ninth
10	ten	10th	tenth
11	eleven	11th	eleventh
12	twelve	12th	twelfth
13	thirteen	13th	thirteenth
14	fourteen	14th	fourteenth
15	fifteen	15th	fifteenth
16	sixteen	16th	sixteenth
17	seventeen	17th	seventeenth
18	eighteen	18th	eighteenth
19	nineteen	19th	nineteenth
20	twenty	20th	twentieth
21	twenty-one	21st	twenty-first
30	thirty	30th	thirtieth
40	forty	40th	fortieth
50	fifty	50th	fiftieth
60	sixty	60th	sixtieth
70	seventy	70th	seventieth
80	eighty	80th	eightieth
90	ninety	90th	ninetieth
100	a/one hundred	100th	hundredth
101	a/one hundred and one	101st	hundred and first

Colours

- red
- orange
- yellow
- green
- blue
- purple
- pink
- brown
- black
- white
- grey
- dark blue
- light blue

Mathematical Symbols

$5 + 10 = 15$
Five plus ten equals fifteen.

$40 - 12 = 28$
Forty minus twelve equals twenty-eight.

$8 \times 7 = 56$
Eight times seven equals fifty-six.

$18 \div 3 = 6$
Eighteen divided by three equals six.

Days

Monday
Tuesday
Wednesday
Thursday
Friday
Saturday
Sunday

Seasons

spring
summer
autumn
winter

Months

January
February
March
April
May
June
July
August
September
October
November
December

Tapescript

Review Unit D In an office
Listening. Exercise 3

Example: The pencils are on the table.
– True.
1 The poster is in the bin.
2 The clock is between the window and the calendar.
3 The telephone is in front of the brochures.
4 The woman is behind the chair.
5 The lamp is on the table.
6 The pencils are near the door.

Unit 1 Arrival
Listening. Exercise 3

MAN: Good afternoon. Can I help you?
TESSA: Yes, my name is Tessa Saunders. I have a reservation.
MAN: Can I have your name again, please?
TESSA: Saunders.
MAN: Oh, yes. A double room with a bath.
TESSA: A double room? No, a single.
MAN: A single? Isn't your husband with you?
TESSA: My husband? I'm not married.
MAN: But we have a reservation here for Mr and Mrs T Sanders . . . Oh, wait, just a moment. How do you spell your name?
TESSA: S . . . A . . . U . . . N . . . D . . . E . . . R . . . S.
MAN: Ah . . . A . . U . . U . . . N . . . D. Not A . . . N . . . D. I'm very sorry, Mrs Saunders. We also have a reservation for Mr and Mrs T Sanders – S . . . A . . . N . . . D . . .E . . .R . . . S. But we have your reservation, too. Ms T Saunders from London. A single room with a shower for two nights. Is that right?
TESSA: Yes. Exactly.
MAN: Your room number is six sixteen.

Unit 1 Can I help you?
Listening. Exercise 2

(The conversation on page 16 continues as below.)

JAMES: Well . . . er, have you got something for about a hundred pounds?
SALESMAN: Hmm . . . come over here, sir. What about this?
JAMES: Hmm. How much is that?
SALESMAN: A hundred and twenty pounds.
JAMES: What's it made of?
SALESMAN: Pure wool.
JAMES: Pure wool?
SALESMAN: Yes, sir. 100 per cent wool.
JAMES: I'm not sure about the colour.
SALESMAN: You don't like this dark blue?
JAMES: No. Have you got it in dark grey?

SALESMAN: I think so, sir. What size are you? 38, isn't it?
JAMES: Yes.

Unit 2 A problem
Listening. Exercise 3

(The conversation on page 20 continues as below.)

TESSA: Hello? David?
DAVID: Yes?
TESSA: The third isn't good for me. What about the day after that?
DAVID: The fourth?
TESSA: Yes, Wednesday, the fourth.
DAVID: Hmm . . . let me see. Just a moment, please. Uh . . . yes, that's all right for me. One o'clock O.K. for you?
TESSA: Yes, one o'clock is O.K. But where?
DAVID: What about the Italian Wine Bar in George Street? Do you know it?
TESSA: Yes, yes. I know it. All right. Let's meet there.
DAVID: OK. Bye.
TESSA: Bye. Hmm . . . I wonder what he wants.

Unit 3 Monday morning
Listening. Exercise 3

JAMES: Excuse me. Can you tell me the way to Blake Street?
POLICEWOMAN: Yes, sir. Go up this street and turn right at those traffic lights.
JAMES: Traffic lights?
POLICEWOMAN: Yes, sir. Up there. Do you see them?
JAMES: Oh, yes. I see them now. Turn left at the traffic lights?
POLICEWOMAN: No, sir. Right. Turn right. Then take the second turning on the left. That's Blake Street.
JAMES: Let's see . . . um . . . I turn right at the traffic lights . . .
POLICEWOMAN: Yes.
JAMES: And then I take the second turning on the left . . .
POLICEWOMAN: That't it.
JAMES: And that's Blake Street.
POLICEWOMAN: Exactly.

Unit 4 What do you suggest?
Listening. Exercise 3

WAITRESS: Can I take your order, please?

YAMADA: Mr Mitchum . . . please go ahead. I'm not sure what I want.

ROGER: All right. I'd like . . . uh . . . let's see . . . yes, the steak, please.

WAITRESS: The fillet steak?

ROGER: Yes.

YAMADA: Don't you want a starter first?

ROGER: Oh . . . uh . . . well, perhaps the seafood . . . no, the fruit cocktail. Yes. The fruit cocktail.

WAITRESS: And for you, sir?

YAMADA: The Pacific salmon, please.

WAITRESS: Oh, I'm very sorry, sir, but I'm afraid there is no more salmon.

YAMADA: No more salmon? Oh. Is there any other fish?

WAITRESS: Our sashimi is very good, sir. We prepare it in a very special way.

YAMADA: Excellent. I always like sashimi. Mr Mitchum . . . are you sure you wouldn't like sashimi?

ROGER: No, thanks . . . uh . . . I'm sure it's very good, but I really don't like fish very much. That's why I'm having the fruit and not the seafood cocktail.

WAITRESS: And vegetables or salad?

ROGER: What are the vegetables?

WAITRESS: Green beans and carrots, sir.

ROGER: Fine.

YAMADA: Only green beans and carrots? Nothing else?

WAITRESS: I'm afraid not, sir.

YAMADA: Then I'd like the salad, with Italian dressing.

Unit 5 No alternative
Listening. Exercise 3

(The conversation on page 32 continues as below.)

RICHARD: I'm afraid the fourth is a very bad day for me. I . . . I can't really be away from the office on that day. However, Tessa Saunders can probably come to Munich then.

KERNHOLZ: Saunders . . . oh, yes. We met her when we were in London.

RICHARD: Yes. In fact, I think it's a good idea for her to learn as much as possible about your company and the new product. She's very important here.

KERNHOLZ: I see. You'd like to send Tessa Saunders. Hmm.

RICHARD: Yes, Herr Kernholz, I would. In fact, I wanted to suggest this idea before.

KERNHOLZ: Yes . . . hmm . . . I think you're right. It's a very good idea.

Unit 6 Plans
Listening. Exercise 2

(The conversation on page 36 continues as below.)

TESSA: Just tell me a little more about this meeting in Munich. I mean, what exactly is it all about?

RICHARD: Their new video camera, of course.

TESSA: Their new video camera?

RICHARD: Yes. It's a new kind of video camera. They plan to sell at least a hundred thousand of them here in Britain alone in one year. Landau talked about that at the beginning of the meeting. Don't you remember?

TESSA: No, I was only at the end of the meeting, not at the beginning. Don't you remember that, Richard?

RICHARD: Oh . . . I forgot. I'm sorry.

TESSA: It's all right.

Unit 7 When do you want to go?
Listening. Exercise 2

Good afternoon, ladies and gentlemen. Flight 263 to San Francisco will be ready to board in a few minutes. We'd like to begin, however, with those passengers with children or who need help to board the aircraft, so if you have children with you or need help in getting on the aircraft, please begin boarding the aircraft now.

Thank you for waiting, ladies and gentlemen. We will now begin boarding the aircraft by seat numbers. Please extinguish all cigarettes or any other smoking materials. We will begin with passengers with green cards sitting in rows forty-five to sixty. Please look at your boarding card. If it is green and if you are sitting in rows forty-five to sixty, please board the aircraft now. Pacific Airways wish you a pleasant flight.

Unit 8 Flying to San Francisco
Listening. Exercise 4

Good evening, ladies and gentlemen. This is . . . um . . . your captain speaking. On behalf of Pacific Airways I'd like to welcome you aboard flight two six three to San Francisco this evening. Our flight time to San Francisco is ten hours and fifteen minutes. The . . . um . . . the time in Tokyo is now seven forty-five in the evening. San Francisco is seventeen hours behind Tokyo time, so that means that . . . uh . . . it is now two forty-five in the morning there. Uh . . . the weather en route is good and we don't expect any delay so . . . uh . . . we expect to arrive on time in San Francisco at twelve fifty. I'll have some information about the weather in San Francisco a little later. I hope you enjoy the flight and I'm sure the cabin staff will do everything possible to make sure that you do. Thank you and . . . uh . . . good evening.

Unit 9 I'd like your opinion
Listening. Exercise 3

(The conversation on page 46 continues as below.)

DAVID: Well, as I said, this is confidential. Very confidential!
TESSA: Yes, I understand. Go on.
DAVID: We're not happy with Bell and Winter, and Nathalie Artaud . . . that's the director of the company (and my boss, of course) . . . Nathalie Artaud wants to find another agency.
TESSA: I see. Hmm.
DAVID: That's why I wanted to see you today. I wanted to find out if you're interested.
TESSA: I see. Hmm.
DAVID: Well, are you?
TESSA: Interested? Yes, David. I'm very interested. But I think I should talk to my boss before I say anything more.
DAVID: Of course.

Unit 10 Away on business
Listening. Exercise 3

CALLER: Hello. This is Graziella Bianchi in Milan. I'd like to speak to Tessa Saunders, please.
PENNY: I'm afraid she isn't here today. She's away on business. This is Penny Miles, her secretary. Can I help you?
CALLER: Well . . . you see, I'm coming to London at the end of this month and I'd like to . . . how do you say . . . arrange an appointment with her.

PENNY: I see. Could I have your name again, please?
CALLER: Graziella Bianchi.
PENNY: Could you spell that, please?
CALLER: G . . . R . . . A . . . Z . . . I . . . E . . . double L . . . A and then B . . . I . . . A . . . N . . . C . . . H . . . I.
PENNY: And when are you coming to London?
CALLER: On the thirtieth. You see, I'm an artist. We met . . . Tessa and I met here in Milan last month and she was interested in my work. I'm bringing some new work with me.
PENNY: Yes, I understand, but before you go on, can you tell me how long you're staying in London?
CALLER: For almost three weeks. From the thirtieth of March to the sixteenth of April.
PENNY: Could I have your number in Milan?
CALLER: Oh, yes. Two seven one six three double four nine.
PENNY: And have you got a number in London where she can contact you, too?
CALLER: Yes . . . just a moment, please. It's . . . uh . . . hello?
PENNY: Yes. I'm listening. Go on.
CALLER: It's oh eight one, four nine seven, six double five seven.
PENNY: Thank you. I'll give her your message as soon as she gets back.

Unit 10 Messages
Listening. Exercise 3

WOMAN: Hello?
ROGER: Hello . . . Could I speak to Anne, please?
WOMAN: She's out. Can I take a message?
ROGER: Uh . . . yes. Just tell her that Roger called.
WOMAN: Roger?
ROGER: Yes . . . oh . . . perhaps she could phone me. I mean, do you know when she'll be back?
WOMAN: Well, she's usually back here by five.
ROGER: Oh. I'll still be in my office then.
WOMAN: So the message is please phone Roger at his office.
ROGER: Yes.
WOMAN: Has she got your number?
ROGER: I think so, but I'll give it to you again. It's four two seven, nine double two zero. Have you got that?
WOMAN: Yeah. Is that all?
ROGER: Yes. Goodbye.
WOMAN: Bye.
ROGER: Oh! Hello? Are you still there?
WOMAN: Yeah. I'm still here.
ROGER: I'm sorry . . . just one more thing. If she

comes back after six, ask her to phone me at home. This evening, if possible. My home number is three seven six, nine six eight one.

WOMAN: Three seven six, nine six eight one. Anything else?
ROGER: Pardon?
WOMAN: Is there anything more you want me to tell her? Are you sure that's the end of the message?
ROGER: Yes. That's all.

Unit 11 It doesn't work
Listening. Exercise 3

KERNHOLZ: How was your flight?
TESSA: Well, there was a delay, but it wasn't very long.
KERNHOLZ: Oh. Well, I'm glad you got here safely. Now, let me introduce you to my colleagues. But of course, you already know Hans Landau.
TESSA: Yes, I do. We met when you and he were in London.
KERNHOLZ: Yes, of course. And this is Barbara Fischer, our publicity director.
TESSA: I'm pleased to meet you.
FISCHER: My pleasure.
KERNHOLZ: Now, uh . . . before we begin the meeting, can we get you some tea or coffee?
TESSA: No, thank you. Later, perhaps.
KERNHOLZ: Good. Let's begin then.

Unit 12 Tomorrow isn't good enough!
Listening. Exercise 3

(The conversation on page 58 continues as below.)

BRADFORD: Where are you going?
ROGER: Out!
BRADFORD: What do you mean?
ROGER: You want the report, don't you? So I'll finish it now. Goodbye!
BRADFORD: Hello? Mary? Listen. This is highly confidential. I don't think Mr Mitchum is going to be our sales manager much longer. So I want you to phone that employment agency . . . uh, what's the name? You know, the one we used last month . . . Yeah, that's right. Well, tell them we're looking for someone with the right qualifications who can start with us in . . . let's say . . . uh . . . three

months time. Have you got that? And remember – this is highly confidential.

Unit 13 Profit and loss
Listening. Exercise 3

(The conversation on page 62 continues as below.)

TESSA: Yes. Thank you very much.
RICHARD: Is seven thirty too early for you?
TESSA: To be at the restaurant, you mean?
RICHARD: Yes.
TESSA: It depends where it is.
RICHARD: It's a new restaurant in Charlotte Street. It's called Picasso's.
TESSA: Charlotte Street. Hmm. Can we make it at a quarter to eight, instead?
RICHARD: All right.
TESSA: And the restaurant is called . . .
RICHARD: Picasso's. P–I–C–A
TESSA: S–S–O apostrophe S. Yes, Richard. The famous painter. Everybody knows that.
RICHARD: Of course. I just thought that perhaps you . . .
TESSA: Do you know the telephone number of the restaurant?
RICHARD: Yes . . . It's here somewhere. Let me see. It's three double five, nine seven four six. Got that?
TESSA: Right. Three five nine . . .
RICHARD: No. Three double five, nine seven four six.
TESSA: Double five nine seven four six. I'll phone you if I think I'm going to be late.

Unit 14 Metro Radio
Listening. Exercise 2

(The conversation on page 66 continues as below.)

PAULA: What are the things you like about your job?
TESSA: Well, first of all, it's very interesting.
PAULA: In what way? How?
TESSA: I learn a lot about the different companies I work with. You see, advertising isn't only about selling products . . . a new video camera or a car, or something like that. It's also important to present an image of the company that makes that product. It's the company's name behind the product that often sells it.
PAULA: Do you travel a lot?
TESSA: Um . . . yes, I suppose you could say so. I go to Germany, Spain, Italy . . . places like that.

PAULA:	And do you enjoy travelling?
TESSA:	I did at first, but I don't enjoy it as much as I did before.
PAULA:	Really? Why not?
TESSA:	I don't like hotels very much.
PAULA:	Oh, yes. I know what you mean.
TESSA:	I don't like staying in them . . . even when they're comfortable first class hotels. I prefer to be at home.
PAULA:	Are there things you don't like about your job?
TESSA:	Yes, I've already told you one. I don't like staying in hotels. And . . . well . . . I don't have time to do some of the other things I'd like to do.
PAULA:	Why is that?
TESSA:	I work long hours . . . often ten hours a day. Sometimes even more than that.
PAULA:	OK, Tessa. Thank you very much.
TESSA:	Pleasure.
PAULA:	Let's have a short break for some music now. Then I'll have some more questions for you.

Unit 15 The usual question
Listening. Exercise 2

(The conversation on page 70 continues as below.)

ANNE:	What about you, by the way?
ROGER:	Me?
ANNE:	Yes. How's your work going?
ROGER:	Uh . . . not so well.
ANNE:	Oh, really? I'm sorry to hear that. Er . . . would . . . would you like to talk about it?
ROGER:	Um . . . I'm not sure if I would.
ANNE:	Oh, I see.
ROGER:	If you really want to know, it's my boss.
ANNE:	Oh . . . you mean you don't like him?
ROGER:	No, that isn't what I mean.
ANNE:	What's the problem, then?
ROGER:	It isn't that I don't like him. I hate him!
ANNE:	Is it that bad?
ROGER:	It's worse than that. I almost quit a few days ago.
ANNE:	Quit? Really? So . . . what do you think you're going to do now?
ROGER:	I don't know . . . but I'll tell you one thing. If he talks to me again the way he did a few days ago, I will quit!

Unit 16 Interested in me? Why?
Listening. Exercise 3

(The conversation on page 74 continues as below.)

RICHARD:	So let's get down to business, Donald. I think you should tell Tessa the most important news.
DONALD:	It's like this, Tessa. There's going to be an important change in the agency.
TESSA:	Oh? What kind of change?
DONALD:	I'm coming to London. You see, I'm going to be director of the London agency. And Richard is taking my job in New York.
TESSA:	But why?
RICHARD:	Family reasons. You know that my children live in America with my ex-wife. Well, I'd like to be closer to them. And anyway, I've been in London now for almost ten years. That's a long time.
TESSA:	So, you're going to be my new boss, Donald.
DONALD:	Well, it depends.
TESSA:	On what?
DONALD:	I'll let Richard explain.
RICHARD:	I'd like you to come with me to New York, Tessa. Would you like to work with me there?
TESSA:	Give up my job here in London, you mean?
RICHARD:	Yes. The pay will be much better.
TESSA:	How much better?
RICHARD:	Five thousand dollars more than you're earning now.
TESSA:	Hmm. I'd like to think about it, Richard.
RICHARD:	Of course.
DONALD:	But I'm afraid we can give you only a week to think about it, Tessa. I hope you understand why.